Behind Her Brand: Entrepreneur Edition Vol. 1

Compiled by Kimberly Pitts

Co-authored by:

Jody Harris

Deb Cantrell

Pam Russell

Marsha Sherrill

Darlene Templeton

Rose Colarossi

Sheryl Jones

Susan Tolles

Yvonne George

Janet Bernstein

Melynda Lilly

Larissa Rubijevsky

Behind Her Brand: Entrepreneur Edition, Vol. 1

Behind Her Brand: Entrepreneur Edition, Vol. 1
1. Business 2. Internet

E-book Version: Kindle
ISBN-10: 0692363548
ISBN-13: 978-0692363546
BUSINESS & ECONOMICS: Entrepreneurship

DEDICATION – THANK YOU

To the many inspired, committed and focused entrepreneurs who have a vision, message, and a clear purpose this book is dedicated to you. The pages were written with you in mind to provide you new perspectives, new approaches and new ways of looking at how you can continue on your entrepreneurial journey.

Thank you to the authors in this book that shared from your heart, your experience and from where you are today. Without your words on these pages, many would not know the blessing it is to be an entrepreneur.

Special thanks to Melva Torres and Jatoya Akinyele without the both of you none of this would have come together. You both are simply amazing and I am so blessed to work with both of you every day.

TABLE OF CONTENTS

Your brand is much more interesting when it has heart and life behind it.

Behind Her Brand is a journey of lessons, obstacles, thought processes, disappointments, victories that you go through when building your business. Creating your brand is much easier when you consciously infuse the breadth and depth of everything you do in what you make, so your experiences nourish your business brand.

Because, guess what?
The story of your brand matters.

Your audience wants to know how you started your business. How you came to be where you are at this very moment. They want to know what you like to do when you're not pounding the pavement with your brilliant work. They want to know about your path --- they want to know the person behind the brand. If they can feel the passion behind your story (and you as a person)? There's a really good chance they are going to trust you with their money.

Each of these authors share their obstacles, victories, and they offer invaluable information that can help you grow, challenge yourself and look at your situations in a new light. I encourage you to learn from their stories and the lessons they have learned along the way to becoming successful entrepreneurs.

To Your Impact and Success,
Kimberly Pitts
Founder, UImpact, LLC & Behind Her Brand

JODY HARRIS
Founder, Zipped Me

First and foremost, I'm a proud mother and a grandmother. My professional career encompasses a successful career as an energy coordinator and a commercial lender. I have never met a challenge I didn't accept which describes my "can do" attitude and my motto "never give up".

This determination prepared me for my entrepreneurial venture where I get to be a problem solver. As the founder and CEO of ZippedMe, I was inspired to simplify women's lives by inventing a product to zip up the back of a dress, zip up your boots or give you the opportunity to be independent while being fashionable.

Tell us a little about yourself. We want to learn about the person behind the brand.

At 16, I found myself pregnant with my daughter, Jenilee. Everyone had turned their back on me. I was told to stay away from my friends because their parents did not approve of me. While my friends were enjoying their teenage years, I was preparing myself for motherhood.

At that point, I made my choice to be the best mother I could be, work hard and never feel sorry for myself. During the next seven years, I would welcome two more precious children: my daughter, Randi Rae and my son, Brice.

However, I was hiding a dark secret. I was in an abusive marriage. As the abuse intensified I feared for my safety and the safety of my children. Therefore, after my son turned three months old I moved out.

I didn't have much, but I had my children and that was all that mattered. Failure was not an option, no matter my age, financial situation or life's adversities. So I reached deep down inside and found my drive. I was going to make my dreams come true. My drive, spirit and hope kept me alive and led me to a successful career and life for my family.

When did you know you were meant to launch your own business?

While away on business, I discovered what a struggle it can be zipping your own dress. One morning I was determined to wear my favorite dress that zipped up in the back. I was struggling to get it zipped. I had tried everything and nothing worked. As I looked in the mirror, I saw a distressed, desperate woman who was running late for a crucial business meeting. I called the concierge desk. After I hung up I thought, "That was a memorable conversation I'm sure will show up as a late night TV skit one of these days.

As I felt my distress growing, I walked out in the hallway. I asked several potential prospects to no avail. Then a mature gentleman walked out of his room, looked at me, smiled and said, "I bet you need help getting zipped?" I smiled and said, "Yes, please!" He zipped me up and said,

"If someone invented something to zip up these dresses they would get rich." At that moment, ZippedMe was born.

Share with us what your business is and why you wanted to start this business.

A week later, I arrived home and shared my damsel in distress story with my family. My family was mortified their mom was asking strangers to zip up her dress. I announced I was going to solve this problem so other women wouldn't have to experience my unzipped, distressed hotel episode.

For me, the process of creating a tool such as ZippedMe begins with trying to solve a problem. I have to analyze the problem from all angles. I start with the problem first. I ask questions such as, Why is it a problem? When does it become a problem? Where is the problem? How is the problem showing up? As I began looking at my responses, I saw a common denominator. If I can't zip up my dress by myself, how do people with mobility issues get zipped up or how does a handicapped person with one arm get zipped up?

Then I asked myself, "When do people encounter these problems? In a hotel? Away on business? At home, wanting to surprise their significant other with being dressed on time? Or just getting dressed by themselves for church on Sunday morning?" These common denominators revealed to me my product needed to be compact, easily accessible and fashionable. Now that I had a vision and my components, I went to work.

First, I started out with a simple raw drawing of what I imagined my product to look like. Then I ventured out to my local hardware and craft store to purchase the components of my product. Shopping for components was not easy for me. I still can see the perplexed faces of those hardware store employees. Next, I needed to build my product's prototype by determining what components were necessary to solve the problem I had identified. Then I had to decorate my prototype so it was appealing to the consumer.

One of my biggest fears was my prototype not working. I remember my first ZippedMe as being a simple but functional product. I was so excited because it solved one problem, my invention zipped up my dress. But what about the other problems I had discovered during the development process? How would it help a person with mobility issues or a handicapped person with one arm? Also, did it look fashionable? If I was in a hurry could I wear it as a necklace?

Reluctantly, I went back to the drawing board. I have to admit this was a challenge for me. I didn't like demolishing and recreating my ZippedMe. But I knew without a doubt I had to make my product functional, so it solved ALL of the identified problems. I also wanted to include charm components to give hope to those who purchased my product. Days turned into weeks. Weeks turned into months. Finally, I created the ZippedMe and this problem-solving accessory was more than I could have ever imagined.

Soon after I invented my product a few of my friends started asking me to make them a ZippedMe because they were struggling to get zipped up for work or for church. A month or two later a friend asked me where she could buy my invention. She wanted to buy them and give them away as Christmas presents. After thinking it over, I realized that if my friends wanted to buy a few ZippedMe's, how many other people would want to buy them as girlfriend gifts, Christmas gifts or birthday gifts? I remember sitting in my office chair holding my invention and saying my problem-solving solution just transformed into a business.

Now things really got serious. I spent months filing legal documents for the business, buying components of my inventory, putting together a manufacturing team and hiring my nephew Matt Lee's company, Lead Generation Experts, to create my website. Then in March 2014, I officially launched ZippedMe and my life has never been the same.

One of the first questions I was asked after launching my company was who manufactures ZippedMe and where is the manufacturer located. I take great pride in telling everyone, my product is manufactured in the United States by hard-working stay-at-home moms, college students or people needing to make extra income to support themselves and their families. I am convinced that right here in my community in Oklahoma we have women and men who need help and want to work. However, their circumstances might not permit the opportunity to work a traditional 9-5 job. Therefore, I structured a manufacturing business model that allows them to be flexible with their time while still meeting my customers' needs. I am proud of my team and their dedication.

Because of my team, my invention is being used around the world. ZippedMe has been in the Las Vegas spotlight, showcased at a red carpet event for the Emmys and named Forbes 2015 Virtual Trendsetter. Who would have thought a "damsel in distress" in a hotel would have invented a product now being sold worldwide. ZippedMe is available through my website and in boutiques across thirteen states and two island resort stores in Puerto Rico and the Bahamas. I am also negotiating with several large department stores.

Each day since I have started this journey, I am thankful. I feel blessed because ZippedMe has created opportunities for my community and my family. It has allowed me to come full-circle by helping people help themselves. During this past year I have been asked the following questions. Some of them really have made me think about my journey and the process of making my dream a reality. My goal is sharing these questions and answers with all of you in the hope they will inspire you to go after your dreams.

How do you measure success and what is your definition of success?

I don't measure my success or my company's success by its financial worth. I measure my success by the goals I have accomplished. If you are in business to make $5 million in the first couple of years, you are creating a false sense of reality for your future. Anyone can go down to their local convenience store and buy a lottery ticket. If you beat the odds and win the jackpot does that make you successful? No, creating and building net worth takes time and patience.

You can create net worth over time while maintaining a decent profit along the way. More than likely, during the next three to four years, you will have established a brand for your business and your reputation will grow. You can measure your business' success based upon increased profits and reduced debt. You also can examine the effectiveness of your marketing, product quality and customer satisfaction. In the end, winning at business means focusing upon what really matters. Your success will be measured by what you do with your company.

What have you learned about yourself in running your business?

First, you are going to make a lot of mistakes when you are starting out. I made several mistakes when I started my business. However, the lessons I learned were instrumental in making my business successful. I thought I would make a problem-solving accessory and customers would come out of the woodwork to buy my ZippedMe's. But that wasn't the case in the beginning. I had to learn to build relationships with my customers. I had to learn what needs they had. I had to learn why they wanted my product. Once

I learned these things my passion, dedication, and purpose came alive.

I never will forget a lady calling a couple of weeks after buying my invention at a trade show. She thanked me for creating an accessory for her daughter, who was born with one arm, because she could use my invention and feel independent while wearing fashionable clothes. When I hung up the phone, my emotions came over me and tears streamed down my face. As I sat on the floor, replaying the phone call in my mind, I told myself, "If I sell one ZippedMe or ten thousand ZippedMe's I never will forget the impact my invention is making in people's lives."

What three things do you wish you would have known when you started?

1.) I wish I would have realized I couldn't make ZippedMe a household name all by myself.

2.) I wish I would have known I needed a network to promote ZippedMe.

3.) I wish I would have known I needed to hire experienced people to make ZippedMe visible.

How do you keep yourself motivated and encouraged when things don't go right?

First and foremost, I take care of myself by exercising at least 30 to 60 minutes a day and taking at least 15 minutes to be alone, closing my eyes and praying. This allows me to refocus and tackle any challenge I run into with energy and passion. Also, I surround myself with an encouraging group. I have a handful of people I trust and use as mentors. We share ideas, challenges and encouragement for all of our businesses.

What's your biggest business goal during the next 12 months and what will you do to meet it?

I want to make ZippedMe a household name. So I am making it a priority to rate each goal and what needs to be accomplished each day, week and month. Goal planning is a necessity for a successful business.

What advice would you give to a woman entrepreneur who is ready to take her business to the next level?

First, you need to take a little time and look at how far you have come on your journey. This step always has been important to me because if you miss this step you could get discouraged. When you take your product or business to the next level your resilience will be tested.

When I started marketing ZippedMe it was difficult to understand that some people didn't want a problem-solving accessory. I had to realize the majority of my customers had to hear about my product at least eight times, while others were sold the first time they saw my invention. Once I came to this realization, I began promoting ZippedMe through different sources, such as social media, magazine advertising, product showcases, podcasts and radio talk shows. Visibility has been a major key to my success.

One of the biggest struggles women entrepreneurs have is how to price themselves. What advice would you share about pricing your services and offerings?

Everything you do has a value. If you are a stay-at-home mom, you have the opportunity to mold your children and watch them grow. You are rewarded by tiny arms that hug your neck and little kisses as they grow older. If you work for a corporation, you have the opportunity to exercise your talents to help promote their business while being paid a salary to financially support your family. As you develop your tenure with a corporation you accept more responsibility and climb the corporate ladder, which gives you more value.

If you are an entrepreneur, you have the opportunity to invent a product or offer a service that is in demand. However, when you begin as an entrepreneur your product or service is in its infancy. Therefore, you have to adjust your value based on demand while still being able to cover your costs. Once your business matures and your brand expands, you will be able to demand more value.

What "must have" resources would you recommend someone use in their business?

Social media is a "must have" resource that will catapult your business into profitability. However, how many of you using social media feel like a fish out of water. The goal of using social media is connecting with new and existing consumers and making your product or service more visible.

The first thing I realized about social media is you have to build momentum. The results don't happen as consistently as we would hope. By focusing on these five items, you not only will be a social media guru, but your social media success will be proven by increased visualization and increased profits.

Branding – Using social media to brand your product or service is crucial. With your content and effort, you can build a reputation for your brand around your company's message and offerings.

Community – Social media allows you to cultivate a neighborhood. Your customers will connect with you emotionally and you will have the opportunity for valuable dialog with them. This type of connection is more powerful than paid marketing research.

Exposure – An old marketing saying is it takes six to eight direct exposures before a customer understands your product or service. Social media allows you to have repeated direct exposures within your network. You have the opportunity to provide your customers with repetitive dialog about how your product or service works and the benefits of buying it. Repetitive exposure will shorten the time before a customer commits to buying your product or service.

Impact – As you build your network, your influence will increase. Once you have a considerable social media audience, it develops a snowball effect. It will draw in new customers, media opportunities and collaborations with partners.

Website traffic – Your social media efforts can lead traffic to your website. By sharing posts, specials and videos, you will generate traffic to your website. You can monitor your traffic by using monitoring software. I use Google Analytics because it generates detailed statistics about the visitors to my website, zippedme.com. It also measures conversions from my social media site to my website.

Many women entrepreneurs are trying to justify the expense and time of handling their social media. Do you spend money hiring someone to promote you on your social media platforms or do you just pick one social media platform and post daily updates? Personally, I do my own posting on social media. I use Socializing, an exciting new, social marketing platform that will help you promote your business on all social media sites, build your network and send out emails and texts all from one place. By focusing on one source for all your social media connections, you have an opportunity to see proven results through increased profits and increased demand for your brand.

Check out my Socializing website at http://zippedme.socialzing.me. It will change the way you view your social media.

What makes you A Woman That Impacts?
How are you impacting your world?

I am a woman who impacts by encompassing my drive, spirit and hope. I am driven because failure is not an option, no matter your age, financial situation or life's adversities. When you reach deep inside and find your DRIVE you will make your dreams come true. My generosity of SPIRIT is helping others in need, whether it is the elderly, handicapped or a woman who needs a job to elevate her life.

My purpose is my HOPE, which is a blessing because it has created opportunities for me to give to my community and my family. My HOPE has allowed me to be a voice for someone who has not found their voice yet.

ZippedMe is a blessed journey.

Continue the Conversation with Jody Harris:

Below are the various ways that you can connect with Jody and learn more about what she has to offer.

Website:
www.zippedme.com

Twitter:
www.twitter.com/zippedme

Facebook:
www.facebook.com/zipmeupplease

Instagram:
www.instagram.com/zippedme

DEB CANTRELL
Founder, Savory Culinary Services

Tell us a little about yourself. We want to learn about the woman behind the brand.

I love being an entrepreneur so much so that I have owned 5 successful companies. I have been a physical therapist for 20 years and after my children were born, I wanted to be with them more, and so I started my very first company, which was a personal chef and catering company. My companies have all been dedicated to healing the body through food and helping busy families to eat together again without stress. My companies have included personal chef, catering, restaurants, commercial kitchens, cooking classes and culinary medicine. I speak all over the country about the healing properties of food to include on stage and in the media. I have been in the culinary field for over 13 years and cannot imagine doing anything else. I simply love everything about food from the way it's grown and the complicated manner in which it hits my palette.

I read once "food can be best medicine or the slowest form of poison." I truly believe that food is a powerful weapon to prevent and dare I say "cure" many common health problems today. Because of this belief, I created an entire company around this concept.

I hear other woman talk about work life balance. I am not even sure what that means. I do know that my family is my first priority and my work is second but balancing the time for both seems to be what we all chase. So I stopped. My family is very supportive of my work and my employees are very supportive of my family time. I do know that my foundation of which I am able to accomplish so much is due to my amazing husband and my biggest cheerleader. This extraordinary man, named Don, puts me back together at times and encourages me to take those giant leaps of faith. He makes me breakfast every morning and runs my bubble bath at night. He truly would love for me to just wake up and he would take it from there. He describes me as a "complete" mess. I usually have food on my shirt from the last amazing meal I savored and my keys and debit card are generally lost. Through the "mess" of me he is always right there. Behind every successful woman is an amazing man. For you ladies reading this, yes he has a brother but that is a different discussion.

The other part of my foundation is my light that I carry with me always. Shelby is my 12-year-old daughter, who hates vegetables anything that even looks like it is going to taste funny. She is a brilliant young lady, destined to for greatness and has a unique practical view about life. I am so honored to be her mother. She has taught me about grace, confidence and iron clad determination. She hopes to be like me one day, or so she says, but in all honestly I want to be like her when I grow up.

My son is 16 years old and I have always joked that he will eat anything that will not eat him first which is pretty much the case and a lot of it. Spencer is a passionate young man who truly has his own way of tackling the world and very much my "why" of starting all of these companies over the past 13 years. The medicinal nature of food has truly changed his life. I have always said that God gave me Spencer to teach me patience and understanding.

My hero is my grandmother who at 93 still lives alone, has an amazing strength and can still make bread better than the most amazing pastry chef anywhere without measuring a darn thing. She is truly the most stoic and strong person I have ever met.

I would be completely remiss if I did not acknowledge my business coach, Allison Maslan. There are no words to ever thank her for all that she has taught me as a business owner but more importantly about myself. All of these people give me my foundation to make a difference in the world and to get up everyday even when I don't feel like it.

Personally, I love to travel, take bubble baths, spend time with family, watch my daughter grow into an amazing young lady, watch my son play football, come home to my dream house, sit on my back porch in my rocking chair and watch the ducks in the pond and deer on the hill. I eat way too much chocolate and probably drink too much wine. I love to watch people truly experience food, life and all of its gifts.

Share with us what your business is and why you wanted to start this business.

My business is called Savor Culinary Services and we transform the lives of our clients and chefs through culinary medicine and conscious food choices one delicious bite at a time. We provide our client's a way to spend more time doing the things they love, stop wasting money at the grocery on the food they buy and will never make, we take the stress of mealtime and improve our client's health on a daily basis. Basically, we make dinner so they don't have to, customize it them and deliver it right to their fridge. We find ourselves doing catering too along the way too. The overall premise of my company is all about conscious food choices and education about what it means to eat "healthy" using pure whole food. The second component of Savor is Culinary Medicine. We focus on helping our client's meet their healthy goals through food sensitivity testing, putting a plan in place that involves nutrition consultation, or a family plan for family's to thrive again despite their food needs, grocery store tours and pantry clean outs or a combination of all of the above.

Thirdly, I created the Culinary Success Institute that consists of programs to guide other chefs and culinary professionals to build culinary businesses around food consciousness based upon their own unique talents as chefs. My brand will soon encompass to companies as the launch of chefdeb.com is in the process now. That company will continue my work around culinary medicine and will include our Culinary Medicine work, the Culinary Success Institute and media relations.

Lastly, I am a speaker and travel the country and speaking to professional women's groups about "Your Bottom Line. How Your Food Affects Your "Ass"ets." This presentation is about educating professional woman how to increase their bottom line in business and personally by changing their thought processes around food and simply taking better care of themselves. The second group that I speak to is professional chef organizations about "How to Make Money in Your Sleep." I am knocking on some very old doors with this presentation because for centuries chefs were taught to stay in the kitchen behind their stoves in their restaurants. I teach chefs to use their intellectual property to make money, build the culinary businesses of their dreams and step outside the box of the traditional chef.

My "why" in business or why I wanted to start my company is because when my son turned 18 months old I noticed there were some things that just were not right. I was told it was poor parenting, he would grow out of it or I needed to put him on medication. Eventually we found out that my son had high functioning autism or severe ADHD. I don't like labels much. What I did know was that I was going to fix this and would do whatever it took to do so.

I spent many years chasing doctors and different treatments. A good friend of mine who is a nutritionist suggested that I have him tested for food intolerances. I decided that it could not hurt. So many food intolerances came back from that test. After many tears, I simply removed those things and he was a different child. Spencer went on to be a straight "A" student and start on the football team. I knew there had to be more kids out there just like him and families struggling just like I was so I created a company to do help other families.

When did you know you were meant to launch your own business?

I can remember being 5 years old standing in my mom's kitchen telling her that I wanted to be a chef when I grew up and she said, "Why? You will never make any money." I remember thinking to myself, "Well…. Why not?"

I have been hard headed my whole life (I prefer goal oriented) and will freely admit it, and since I was told that I would not succeed that bothered me A LOT. Fast forward several years and I needed a way to stay home with my kids and still make money. I was reading a Cooking Light magazine one day while working out and read about being a personal chef. I realized that I could cook for my clients during the day while my son was at school and my daughter could go with me to my client's homes.

I realized I had the opportunity be around food all day and be with my kids. With my daughter on my hip, off I went to cook. Evidently I was damn good at this business thing because 1 client turned into 5 clients and 5 clients turned into 40 clients with a restaurant, personal and catering business at one point. I was hooked when I realized that I could make as much money as I wanted to and did not have to wait any longer for someone to share theirs with me. I could not stand that someone else was deciding my value and putting a dollar sign on that. I found a way to be a chef, make money and stay home with my children. I have launched 5 other companies since that first small personal chef company and have helped countless others do the same. It seems

What has been in business for yourself done for you? Where do I begin?

There are obvious things that being in business has done for me. It has allowed me to be there for my children and not miss a thing. It has allowed me to control my own schedule and decide what I am worth and get paid for it without having to share it with anyone or anything else. Honestly, being in business has taught me things I was not expecting.

Owning your own business is hard - really hard. It is not for weak-minded people who lack confidence and avoid risks. In fact, you have to be part crazy to want to do this. It feels like riding a motorcycle sometimes 100 miles an hour with no protective gear in a bikini. You are completely vulnerable and exposed. In fact when I was attending a workshop there was a quote that said the reason why companies fail is because the owner simply quits.

This experience has truly taught me what I am made of. I would not be the woman I am today had not I taken those scary, breath taking, make you want to throw up leaps of faith that you have to take in business in order to grow. I truly know that I can accomplish anything that I want to.

There is no safety net in owning your own business. Each step you take is scarier than the next sometimes. There are days when I am on my knees praying, so frustrated I have no idea what to do. Other days, I am amazed at the lives I change and the things I can accomplish. Sometimes all of these things happen in the same day. I truly love owning my own business and can never go back to someone's version of me.

If someone asked you, who are your ideal clients, what would you say?

I have two components of Savor, which can be called the "Eaters" and the "Feeders." A name so lovingly give to my two target clients by my VMO's (Chief Marketing Office) son Mr. Joey Lucente. The first component is a B-to-B component, which is my Culinary Success Institute (the Feeders) in which I teach chefs to develop, and up level their own culinary business based upon conscious food education and their own unique gifts. My ideal client is a chef or culinary professional who has been in business for at least 1 year or has owned another business and is ready to start a culinary business. This person generally is stuck in their current business and has no clue how to take it to the next level or is tired of not making the money they deserve. My clients for the Culinary Success Institute want to truly make a difference in their client's lives, typically loves food, does not want to open a restaurant but wants to express their talents in the food industry and serve their clients in their own way.

Secondly (the eaters), I have my B to C component of my business, which includes my personal chef services, catering, and culinary medicine program. My ideal client for this component is a busy family or individual that that wants to eat healthy or has a health concern (special dietary need) and does not have the time or does not like to cook. My clients in this category generally enjoy food and some even love to cook but because life gets in the way they need help in this area. Who would not want dinner prepared just for them and delivered straight to their fridge? Dinner and dishes are done in 20 minutes.

How do you measure success and what is your definition of success?

I measure success by having the money in the bank to travel when and where I please. I am able buy the things I need and some of the things I want. My bills are paid without effort and a growing savings account with well thought out investment strategies that will allow me to retire when I choose to and a college fund for my kids. All of that sounds very boring and textbook. Although there is some honesty to it, really the definition of success is an evolving living thing. I don't think anyone truly knows how to measure it. My goal is to keep doing this business until I don't any longer. Pure and simple.

My daughter wrote me a note one day and said, "Mom, I am so proud of you for all that you have accomplished." I am leading by example and she is proud of me. Therefore, my most important job on the face of this planet has been accomplished. In her eyes, I am her hero. SUCCESS.

My definition of success may be different than most. I don't have a definition for it as I mentioned earlier. I set very high goals in my business and for myself each year and then when they are met I set even higher goals. I really think goals are merely guidelines and best guesses that should be used a path meant to be altered and not a blueprint that must be followed. It is very hard for me to know when I am successful or have reached my goal because I constantly strive for more and try to take advantage of new opportunities that deviate me from my path. Most would say I fly by the seat of my pants. I make decisions very quickly for better or worse. Other people have said that I run a successful business and I am a success, but I will always reach further and higher which means I will never know my pinnacle of success. I truly feel this business is one of my purposes in life and since I was given the strength and the talent for what I do that I should honor that gift to the best of my ability.

What was the biggest obstacle you've encountered since being in business? How did you overcome it?

The biggest obstacle I have encountered since being in business is that I had to get out of my own way. I kept trying to save money and do it all myself. I could not image hiring anyone because it was hard to let go of the money. I realized that I needed to stay in my "Zone of Genius" and allow others to be in theirs. Whatever it was that I needed help with was done better, faster, less painful and normally less money. I also realized I was not taking big enough leaps. Playing it safe will get you nowhere in business.

I have learned the art of delegation and seek people out that will help me solve my problem. I always hope to find someone better than me in all areas of my business. Once I realized that if I charge $100 an hour and I could pay someone $10 an hour to do the things I was pulling my hair out about then I just made $90. On the other hand, I could lose $90 to by doing that $10 an hour job. I also realized that sometimes you have to invest in really good people that charge what they are worth in order to reach your goals like a business coach.

I overcame my fear of letting go of money and hiring other people for what they do best because I had stopped growing. I was literally at capacity with clients and was frustrated that I could not serve more. I only had one choice. It was so scary at first to allow others to care for my dream and something I had worked so hard to build. Letting go is VERY hard. Eventually, we all reach a point where there is not a choice and we come to a crossroads where we either "Go big or go home."

What have you learned about yourself in running your business?

Running my own business has taught me so many things about myself. Where do I begin? I have realized that I have unlimited earning potential and that I am capable of making as much money as I would like to in my business. A good friend of mine said that "as an entrepreneur if you more money you just go and make it." Never again will anyone else decide how much I am worth by sharing his or her money with me. I decide how much I am worth and then ask other people to pay accordingly and they do. That is priceless.

I have also learned that I am extremely goal oriented and can see a future way behind what others can see. Someone asked me not long ago if I knew I would be this successful and without hesitation I said "yes." I even surprised myself. I knew I was driven and goal oriented but I had no idea that I would find myself with a belief system that I could literally do and accomplish anything.

I have invested a great deal of money and lost a great deal of money and yet I continue. I have learned that when things seem to go wrong in my company that it is simply showing me the wholes that need to be fixed. It used to devastate me when a great employee would leave but now I understand that space is being cleared for someone amazing that needs to step into that spot to further improve my company. I knew I was driven and goal oriented in the past, but owning my own business made me realize that I have relentless iron clad determination. I have also learned to have complete faith because someone that is all there is.

What was your most rewarding experience since starting your own business?

The most rewarding experience since starting my own business actually has to do with the clients that I serve and nothing to do with me. One example would be a family that I was working with several years ago. They had a young child with autism and were exhausted with traditional medicine. They had taken him all over the world to be treated, poked, prodded and examined by many different health care providers. They decided that since they tried everything else that now they would try to change his food.

We started with food allergy testing and I referred them to a nutritionist friend of mine for supplementation to assist his body in healing. We set up an eating plan for them and a path for them to follow. One day I came into the home and the mom had tears in her eyes. She said, I heard "I love you, mom" for the first time her life. Nothing can replace that. I knew from that point on that I was chosen for this work and that I had found my true passion. I have been told the two most important days in your life are the day you were born and the day you find out why? I found out why that day and have again and again.

What 3 things do you now wish you would've known when you started?

The three things that I wish I would have known when I started was that you cannot do it all alone. You must hire a team as quickly as possible, even if you feel like you don't have the money. The money will come. I had no idea that I was actually losing money by trying to do it all myself.

Secondly, at some point you will have to invest money, way more money, than you are comfortable with in order to grow. Eventually, everyone gets to a point where they beat their head against the wall enough that they have nowhere else to go but to invest to grow your business. It is always smart to reinvest in your own company, but I am talking about really investing in your company, which truly means investing in yourself to the point where it makes you nauseated and you have to borrow money or find investors. If you don't invest in yourself or your company, how do you expect your clients to invest in your services?

Thirdly, I wished that I would have known the importance of hiring a coach or a mentor. My profits tripled and I grew as a person when I did so. Allison (my business coach) helped me to understand the power of mindset and pushing myself further than I thought possible.

How do you keep yourself motivated and encouraged when things don't go right?

When things are not going well, I have learned that there is usually something going on inside me. When my company is out of control, clients are cancelling their service, my employees are unhappy, no business is coming in and the whole world just seems to be in chaos, I have come to realize that I need to look directly inside me and what I am putting out into the world.

I tell my kids "what you give to the world you get from the world." When this happens, I try and go away alone for a few days or even just a few hours to a very quiet place like the botanical gardens or the beach. I walk and analyze exactly what is happening inside me. Once I wrestle with that and figure out what the turmoil is, I then choose something positive to repeat and live by. In the past what has worked really well was, "I have consistent, happy and abundant clients." I live that mantra, write it everywhere and will not allow myself to believe anything else.

The very next day the phone starting ringing, my employees came in with better attitudes and my business starts rocking again. I practice this so much that now that I can recognize the colossal train wreck that is about to occur and stop it before it starts.

Mindset is a very powerful tool and what you put out in the universe, it will be returned either positive or negative. I also surround myself with like-minded successful people in a few mastermind groups that I am a part of. It really helps at times to just pick up the phone and simply say, "I need your help." As strong women, it is really hard to do that. This group of ladies offers support and a strong kick in the pants when needed. My husband is one of my biggest cheerleaders and at times the only person that can snap me out of my negative mindset and help me to see objectively what is going on.

What's your biggest business goal over the next 12 months and what will you do to meet it?

I have never had just one big business goal. I generally have 3 to 4 big business goals that I work on for the year. Next year I will first and foremost, take better care of myself through consistent workouts, setting strong boundaries of time and my general overall health. As far as business, I have definite revenue goals with the exact number of chefs that I want in my coaching programs at all 3 levels. Since I created this revenue stream, I have not been able to explore each level as deeply as I wish and set up a strong foundation for each level.

The next goal is to develop the Chef Deb.com. I have hired an amazing branding expert, a website is being developed and copy written. This will involve national exposure by various speaking events and multiple videos carried through social media.

Lastly, I plan on offering a new product of cold press juices and smoothies that will need to be introduced to the world and marketed successfully. I have financial goals around this offering as well and numbers that I want to hit. In order to meet these above goals successfully, I have already started to hire a bigger team of the right people that share my vision and mission to include experts in each area to help me achieve my goals. I have learned to write down the details of my goals to include date I will accomplish them by and the money that I will make with each one of them.

What advice would you give to a woman entrepreneur who is ready to take her business to the next level?

The best advice I could give a woman entrepreneur is to take her business to the next level is to invest in a business coach. It seems like everyone these days that are out of work is trying to be a business coach. It took me 2 years to find the one I use. I wanted her to truly live, what she taught. Hiring my coach allowed me to triple my business in a year. She taught me about the importance of mindset and I still use those teachings every day to continue to thrive in my business. She truly taught me to value my expertise and that I have to charge what I am worth. As a result of her, I developed revenue streams that will consistently serve me and help me to further grow my business.

The second advice I would give it to hire someone to help as soon as possible, even if you feel like you do not have the money. I heard a statistic that stated "people that hire other people to help within the first 6 months of opening their business make it to a million a great deal faster." It is so hard to let go of the money, but once you do, you will wonder how in the world you ever did it without help. Figuring out how to do a brain dump to the person is the hardest part because it will slow you down for a few days.

One of the biggest struggles women entrepreneurs have is how to price themselves. What advice would you share about pricing your services and offerings?

In the past, I have had clients constantly try and negotiate my price, and I would give in and lower it. I would shy away or feel guilty about asking for the price that I knew I should be asking for and deserve to get. I have come to realize that if I change my prices based upon my customer's reaction, then I devalue my service and myself. I have learned to stand up for what I know I should be charging and be proud of it. If I were to take jobs or clients for lower than what I know I should be charging, then I would attract the client's that will constantly want me to charge a lower price. I promise you. It does work that way. I have learned to stand up for how good I am and to charge what I know I should charge.

How do you feel when you take less than you know you should? You feel like you sell your soul a little. Taking clients out of desperation leads to always taking clients out of desperation. I practiced in front of mirror until I got it right. I have been in business for over 13 years and I am still astounded that people pay this much for food but then again, I can do food and they cannot. I would be just about paid anything if my computer were broken to make it work again.

It is all about pain points. You have to find theirs at the very beginning of your conversation and speak to that. If they haggle over your price, do not lose credibility by lowering it you can lessen the service you provide but not your price. What happens when you go to buy something and the person sitting in front of you gives you a price? You stop and think, and they lower it without even giving you a chance to respond. You just lost faith in them. It works the same way in any industry and with your service.

What must have resources would you recommend to use in your business? My must have resources include:

Google Analytics – This is a free invaluable tool that really helps me to analyze my website and Pay per Click campaigns. I keep tabs on where my visitors from my website are coming from so I know what geographic locations to market in. It also tells me which pages on my site people are visiting or not visiting so that I can remove the pages that no one visits and really focus on those that they are visiting. I can also tell where my visitors come from in terms of social media as well. If my visitors come from Facebook more than LinkedIn and I spent a great deal of time on LinkedIn then I know to change my focus.

Infusionsoft – Is an invaluable sales and marketing software. It allows is my CRM management system, shopping cart and the sales funnel process is done for you. "Campaigns" are set up for each offering that you have and then your listed is nourished through those campaigns. It can be set up in such a way that if a client clicks on an email Infusionsoft will nourish them until they open the email and then a different path is started. It is quite the investment at first and normally you will have to have someone run it for in which there are partners but so worth it.

QuickBooks – QuickBooks has certainly streamlined my bookkeeping process from accounts payable, to account receivables, to invoicing, merchant services and keeping up with my numbers every month. I especially love that I can pull it up on my phone and do anything I need to do from there.

Dropbox – Dropbox is a great file sharing system. It saves my company so much time because each employee can go to one place to find information about each client or various forms we use. There is an app for the phone where we can gain access very easily. We can all place information into a client folder and see updates from there.

Leadpages.net – Leadpages is a great new program that I have recently started using. I started needing lead pages for many of my offerings such as personal chef services, gift certificates, special joint venture events, etc. And was having difficulty building a landing page around each one from my website. Lead pages has several easy to use and tested templates to simply drag and drop your information into them. It also splits A/B testing to make to compare 2 campaign's performance. Lead pages have done a great deal of research to make sure their pages are high converting and it is less than $30 to join.

Odesk – O desk has become a great site to find help with all kinds of tasks that require an expert to tackle such as graphics, logos, website, reports, proofreading and editing.

Anything you can do on a computer from graphic design, simple blog posts or software development can be done by freelancers who bid on your project and charge reasonable prices. This is great for an adjunct to a seasoned business or for a startup.

What makes you a Woman That Impacts?

How are you impacting your world? When I was 5 years old I can remember standing in my mom's kitchen while she was cooking. I can remember the smells in the kitchen and the feel of the harvest gold linoleum beneath my feet. I looked up at my mom and I told her that I was going to be a chef one day. Her response. "Why in the world would you ever want to do that because you will never make any money."?

When I graduated from high school, I decided to be a physical therapist. While I loved practicing physical therapy something was always calling me to heal people through food. I have successfully built 5 companies and working on my 6th around a simple notion of healing people through food and food consciousness. All of my revenue streams either feed or teach consumers or chefs about the healing power of food. I have seen cancer reverse, diabetes cured and lives changed by doing one thing…. Food. Ann Wigmore said it best, "The food you eat can either be the safest and most powerful form of medicine or the slowest form of poison." I change the world. One bite at a time.

Continue the Conversation with Deb Cantrell:

Chef, dietary consultant, sought after public speaker and mentor to other culinary professionals. She and her team specialize in helping those who are facing food allergies, food sensitivities and/or specific dietary requirements due to disease or other medical diagnosis. She accomplishes this through customized meal delivery and food sensitivity testing with a national reach and education through global online education as part of her Culinary Medicine offerings. Trained at the Culinary Business Academy, Fort Worth Culinary Institute and the Culinary Institute of America, Deb is a senior certified personal chef (CPC®) and boutique caterer.

Below are the various ways that you can connect with Deb and learn more about what she has to offer.

Website:
www.thesavorchef.com

Twitter:
www.twitter.com/savorculinary

Facebook:
 www.facebook.com/savorculinary
www.facebook.com/DebCantrell

PAM RUSSELL
Founder, The Be Influence

Tell us a little about yourself. We want to learn about the person behind the brand.

I am a native Texan, and I say y'all. I don't ride a horse to work. I'm also a native Dallasite. That's a rare combination. I'm a single mom, a dog lover, a passionate volunteer in the memory care unit of a local nursing home. I love purses and shoes. I've never met a stranger. I meet new friends everywhere. Grocery store. Post office. Best Buy. The bathroom. I'm a people person.

I am a fan of humor and enjoy making people smile and laugh. It is probably what my friends would say first when asked about me. That I am funny and fun to be around.

I have had an award winning and successful career as an account executive (sales) for almost 20 years. Eleven of those years working for someone else and nine for myself. It fits in with my love of people. I love the sales process and inspiring others to succeed at it. It doesn't have to be hard.

I have experienced many ups and downs in my life. None of which I would change. They have all made me who I am today and have landed me smack dab in the middle of my passion and purpose. It's hard to see that when you are going through difficult and painful experiences. That all of it has a purpose.

I believe everyone has value and influence to bring to the world based on their own unique experiences and expertise. I strive to live my life believing the best will come to pass. My faith will be my eyes. Being me is the best me to be. And that being vulnerable and courageous is a liberating and fabulous place to reside.

Share with us what your business is and why you wanted to start this business.

My business is about living my passion and my purpose and equipping and inspiring other women to do the same. *I empower women to discover and clarify their purpose. I equip them to monetize it so they can live their passion and be inspired to influence others in the process. I believe that everyone has value to bring from the perspective of their resume, experience and expertise. Often times it takes a third party to be able to give a person a vision for what that would/could look like for them. I help them to see the Big Vision. Then I walk them through the process of breaking that vision down into manageable steps so they can achieve their dream.*

I wanted to start this new part of my business after I went through the exact process and experience. Coming out of a decade long residence in grief and then being transformed and delivered to a place I never thought I would be. A place where I discovered that your pain can deliver you to your purpose. I know I am not alone. I'm not the only one with pain in my past. Their purpose may be waiting for them because of it too. I inspire women to walk through it, see it, believe it and then live it!

Another part of my business involves equipping entrepreneurs and rookie salespeople to be successful in sales. To be equipped with the basics so that they can succeed and not struggle in their business. I struggled for years when I started in sales. No direction. No training. Sales does not have to be a dirty word. It can be a fun and engaging experience when done in a unique and interactive manner. My desire is to empower women, you, to Be Visible in business, Be Equipped to succeed and Be Inspired to influence.

When did you know you were meant to launch your own business?

I knew I was meant to launch my own business the year after my parents died. In 2004. I had been in the promotional products industry as an account executive for about a decade. I national well known franchise organization had been after me to come on board and open a franchise with them. I said no. Over and over again. My answer was no because I liked the security of working for a 'company'. So I thought.

After my parents died a few days apart reality started to sink in over the following months. Life is short. A company, for me, was not my security. So I said yes. Yes to my own business and I haven't looked back. I wouldn't have it any other way now. It's not for everybody. But if it is for you, or you want to find out if it is, I say go for it. Life is short. No regrets.

What has being in business for yourself done for you?

My first thought is that 'done for you' can mean different things to different people. For me it means what has it done for my quality of life. Two things come to mind right away.

Flexibility. It has provided me with an enormous amount of flexibility. I don't mean flexibility as in now I can do a backbend. I mean in my life. With my time. Flexibility as a single mom for many years. Flexibility to be there for my daughter for school programs, when she was sick, picking her up from school every day before she could drive herself.

Flexibility to help others. Flexibility to be present when I otherwise may have not been able to do so. Flexibility to be flexible. It has been a very valuable piece of the owning my own business puzzle. I have learned how to balance being flexible with being successful. Not everyone can do that because they want to say yes to flexibility more than putting in the work to be successful. It's a fine line.

Relationships. I have had the opportunity to meet some amazing people on this journey. People I would have likely never met otherwise. I meet new people almost every day. Some I do business with and some I don't. Some in both of those categories have become dear friends. People, relationships, are a huge benefit to being in business. Relationships are the oil to the engine of business... and life.

If someone asked you, who are your ideal clients, what would you say?

I have two ideal clients:

Rookie Salesperson. This can include entrepreneurs (many don't realize that they are in sales). This can include rookie salespeople in the corporate world. I struggled for years when I started in sales. No direction and no one to train me. Just thrown out there and told to sell. I have a passion for inspiring and equipping the rookies to succeed so that they don't struggle the way I did in the beginning. I want them to hit the ground running with basic knowledge about prospecting, sales conversations, proposals and relationship building. So they can SUCCEED.

Women. My other ideal client is women. Women that have been in the corporate world and now want something different. Women that have an incredible resume, but don't know what to do with all experience and expertise. How to move with that into the entrepreneurial world. OR help them see new opportunities within the corporate environment. For years I have helped my family and friends walk through this transition with great success from the perspective of their resume, experience and expertise. I have 20/20 BIG VISION. There are options and choices to monetize and live your passion and purpose.

How do you measure success and what is your definition of success?

Success to me is being happy and passionate about what I do every day. How I do it. And who I do it with. Truly living my calling, my purpose. It's about seeing the "ah ha" moments on my clients' face when she gets it. When she finally realizes that she has value to bring from the perspective of her resume, experience and expertise. That she does have new opportunities within or outside her current space in life and business.

I have learned that success does not always mean the amount of money in the bank. Success is also about the difference you make in someone's life. That is priceless. Sometimes success means being able to stay in business one more year. Or helping others achieve success. Or helping someone see their own opportunities for success. Success is delivered via many different vehicles.

"Success is liking yourself, liking what you do and liking how you to it." ~Maya Angelou

What was the biggest obstacle you've encountered since being in business? How did you overcome it?

My biggest obstacle has really been three obstacles. Me, myself and I. Triplets. My thoughts. My limiting beliefs. The voice in my head.

The voice that says, "Who do you think you are? Why would you think that someone would want to hire you to...?"

Most of that happened, honestly, on social media. People, friends and competitors posting everything they were doing in their business and life. Speeches, travel, workshops, vacations, etc. It may seem silly, but I started to feel that I was less than because of seeing and reading those things. Less successful. Less worthy. Less creative. Less valuable. Less many things.

I overcame it when I realized that I have my own path to walk in my business and in my life. It looks different than their path. It looks different than your path. It should. I can't lock myself into that comparison prison that we can create for ourselves. I was comparing my speaking and coaching business to businesses/people that have been doing it for years... many years. Doing the comparison thing will keep you twisted up and stuck...and likely broke. Stop and walk your own path.

I overcame it when I hid, stopped following, disconnected on social media from those that made me feel that way. Not because they are bad people. Not because I didn't like them. I did it to protect my thoughts. Protect Pam. Yes, I clicked the button. The unfollow button. Not the unfriend button. The unfollow button. I know social media can turn into a high school like circus really quick but you have to do what you have to do to stay focused on you and your path. Distractions, detours and dimmed progress can be destructive and detrimental to your success. Do what you need to do to keep the eye on the prize. Your prize. Your path. Your success.

I overcame it when I was me. When I was Pam... full out. When I realized that not everyone is a fit for everyone in business. YOU will attract people that being you attracts. YOU will repel people that being you repels. I don't mean repel in a bad way. I mean repel as in not your ideal client. There is enough business for everyone.

Trying to serve everyone will keep you exhausted and frustrated. Trying to be something, someone, which is not true to you is one of the hardest things you will ever try to do. A friend told me once that I needed to bring my humor down a notch. Based on that one person's opinion, I tried to bring it down a notch. To not be me. To be someone I am not. It was excruciating to try to do. Choosing to be YOU is the easiest thing you will ever do. Try to do that and things will fall into place.

"Today you are You - that is truer than true.
There is no one alive who is Youer than You."
~Dr. Seuss

What have you learned about yourself in running your business?

I have learned many things about myself over the last almost decade of owning my own business. Some good and some not as good. I have learned from all of them.

Security. As I mentioned above, I put off the offers to own a franchise for many years. I had the idea that working for a company was my security. Now I see that security comes from other sources. One of them for me is taking consistent action in growing my business. Consistency is my security. Not working for someone else's company.

Strength. I have learned that I am stronger than I thought. That I have the strength to do things that scare me and things that challenge me. I have learned that strength comes from different experiences and challenges. Overcoming and failing. Defeat and success. All things that are part of owning and running a business. In the end all of them will build you up and make you a better person and a better business.

Self. I have learned to be myself. Be Pam. Not someone else's idea of what Pam should be but who I am. To the core who I am. My business is about my passion and purpose. I have almost 20 years in a successful sales career. It seemed logical that I when I thought about moving into the coaching world that I would be a Sales Coach. Sales coaching is part of my business, but it's not the only part of my business. I have learned that I can do and not do what I do and do not want to do. Happiness is the goal.

What was your most rewarding experience since starting your own business?

My most rewarding experience since starting my business, is the example I have set for my daughter. The example that she can be a business owner if she chooses to be one. She can live her passion and purpose. She can achieve anything that she sets her mind to on a consistent basis. She can be her own boss. Or not be her own boss. She can be an entrepreneur and succeed at living her dream. Or she can do that by working for someone else. She has watched me transition from working for someone else to owning my own business. She has witnessed my business changing from time to time. Hard times. Prosperous times. She has choices. She chooses.

"I love my mother as the trees love water and sunshine. She helps me grow, prosper, and reach great heights." ~Terri Guillemets, Quotation Anthologist

What 3 things do you now wish you would've known when you started?

My path. Walk your path, not someone else's path. We can get caught up in what others are doing around us and think that we should be all of that too. Maybe some of it we should be doing. Other parts of it might not be a fit for our own path. Stay focused and committed to what you feel is right for you regardless of what you see around you.

Plan to succeed. I'm not sure if you are like me or not... but when I knew I wanted to start the new part of my business, the sales coaching and purpose and clarity strategist business, I already had a business I was running at the time. My printing and promotional products business.

That business seemed to always take precedence over developing the new business. Time went on and on and on and no progress in developing the new business. That is not a plan to succeed.

Block time in your schedule, each week, to work on developing your business. New parts of your business. Your new business. Whichever one pertains to your situation. Otherwise a year will go by and you will still be wishing, dreaming and hoping to do it someday. Plan to succeed.

Give yourself permission. This was a huge one for me. As I mentioned above, I deferred developing the new part of my business because I already had a business that I was involved in every day. Every day for the last almost ten years. I was used to being involved in it every day. My 'new' division was not producing income yet, so I didn't think I should be working on it during the day per se, during 'work hours". That work should be done in the evening or the weekends. Let me just say that mindset will deliver exhaustion and burn out. Burn out for anything business.

Finally, I had an "ah ha" moment. I finally realized that I had to give myself permission to work on my new business during the day. This is true even if you are just starting to develop a business at all. From scratch. Either way, give yourself permission to work on your dream. One step at a time, so you can see it come to fruition. See it become a reality.

How do you keep yourself motivated and encouraged when things don't go right?

Being an entrepreneur for a decade will teach you a few things about being an entrepreneur. There will be things that don't go right. In life and in business. I have come to realize that some things just aren't going to go right. I have also come to realize that many things don't go right for a reason. Although that doesn't mean I get to that place right away. I get discouraged and frustrated when things don't go as planned just like the rest of the world. I try to remember to do the following when that happens:

Evaluate. Evaluate the situation and try to view it from a higher level. See what, if anything, could have been done differently or better. Evaluate what may have been forgotten or what may have been too much.

Learn. Learn from any mistakes you may have made and vow to make necessary changes next time. I always try to remind myself that when things are not going right, it always teaches me something. Something to do. Something not to do. It's all good. Live and learn.

Call a friend. Sometimes you just need to have a good cry and/or let it all out. The disappointment if you are feeling it. The discouragement. The frustration. Whatever you need to let out. Nothing better than a chat with a girlfriend that understands to let it all out. I have done it many times. It's girlfriend code, right? Must be willing to listen to and endure crying at times. Give someone a call, talk it out and let it go.

Remember that things can go wrong so that other things can go right. You might not see it right away, but you will likely see it down the road. These things have helped me tremendously. They have kept my head on straight and kept me moving forward.

"Sometimes when things go wrong it's because they would have turned out worse if they had gone right." ~Mark Amend, Author of "Lines of Thought by an Unknown Author"

What's your biggest business goal over the next 12 months and what will you do to meet it?

At the end of each year I like to choose a word that will be my theme for the next year. I got the idea from a friend of mine. My word for 2014 was TRUST. Trust ended up being the perfect word for me in 2014. Trust in my direction and path in rebranding my business. Trust in what I could feel but not see... yet. Trust to take the next step. My word for 2015 is CONSISTENCY. It relates to my big goal for 2015. To be consistent. To follow my own coaching advice and be visible...consistently.

- Be visible consistently.
- Be present consistently.
- Be intentional consistently.
- Be committed consistently.
- Make progress consistently.
- Take one step at a time consistently.

I have a detailed plan to achieve this that I won't go into here. It will happen. At the end of 2015 I fully expect to look back on the previous twelve months and see that I achieved the expectations I placed upon myself by choosing that word. Consistently consistent.

What advice would you give to a woman entrepreneur who is ready to take her business to the next level?

I would encourage her to go for it. I would encourage her to make sure she knows what that next level is, where it is, what it looks like, and how she plans to get there. I would encourage her to schedule time each week to make sure she is taking steps towards that next level. I would encourage her to monitor her progress and celebrate achievements along the way to getting there.

Monitoring your progress will allow you to look back at the successes along the path that will encourage you when you might get down during the journey to that next level. Keep your eye on the prize. On your goal. You may have to redirect some of the steps, but the goal should stay the same. Onward and upward!

"Dreams come true when desire transforms them into ACTION."
~Quote from Napoleon Hill's book Think & Grow Rich

One of the biggest struggles women entrepreneurs have is how to price themselves. What advice would you share about pricing your services and offerings?

The advice I would give her is to not undervalue your experience and expertise. Just because you have been doing something in a certain way for years and it has delivered success for you – does not mean others know how to do it that way. I learned this about several of the systems I created and have used throughout my sales career.

When I started doing sales coaching I discovered that people found value in my prospecting techniques and how I conducted sales conversations. YOUR systems, techniques, experience and expertise deliver value to others. Price them as such. When you are considering what to charge someone you have to evaluate it based on THEIR perspective. What value they will get from it not how you see it.

The processes you have used for years that contributed to your success, other people want to know and learn from them. If you under value your expertise others will too. Do you want to be the blue light special or the golden ticket to their success? Price accordingly.

What must have resources would you recommend to use in your business?

Books. Business books. Inspirational books. How to books. Humorous books. So much can be learned from books. You can be inspired by books. You can be equipped by books. You can succeed by reading books. Words on paper can deliver so much. Turn the pages or scroll on a screen. Read books.

> *"Not all readers are leaders, but all leaders are readers." ~Harry S. Truman*

Help. Hire help in the areas that are not in your zone of genius. I wish I had learned this long before I did. Actually, I did learn it, but I was too afraid to spend the money to do it. Wrong choice. Do it when you might be afraid to do it. I spent way too much of my time trying to do things that are not my expertise. I should have done it way before I did it.

Trying to save a dime will cost you a dollar... or more. Step out and do this when you feel the time is right for you. My first hires were a Virtual Assistant that was an expert in my email management system and a graphic designer. I didn't hire them as W-2 employees. I hired them as a service provider. They bill me each month and I pay them each month. Invest what you can as soon as you can. Hiring resources to do the things that are not your gifting will help catapult your success. It will be so worth it!

Email Management System. Most businesses will need to communicate via email. It helps to have a system that can send email campaigns and provide data so you can evaluate your email marketing efforts. Otherwise, it is just a guessing game on what is and what is not working. There are inexpensive options for when you are just starting out and more detailed and expensive options for when your list begins to grow.

Coaching. I believe every business owner, even coaches, need a coach. A coach can be a great asset to your business growth and success. There are many different kinds of coaches out there. Business Coach. Life Coach. Social Media Coach. Marketing Coach. All kinds. Evaluate what your needs are, research them and make a decision. Coaching should be an important component of your business plan.

What makes you a Woman That Impacts? How are you impacting your world?

I believe I am impacting the world by empowering women to be who they are. To do different things. See different possibilities. To be the best YOU they can be. With my humor, inspiration and my expertise in seeing the big vision and the success that awaits them. I hope that I am inspiring women to be bold, vulnerable and courageous. To tell their story. To live their passion and purpose. That they matter. That they have their own impact to live, breathe and share with the world!

Continue the Conversation with Pam Russell:

Pam Russell is an award winning sales professional, author and popular and energetic speaker. She has an infectious personality and enjoys inspiring others to succeed in monetizing their passion and purpose. She is a native Texan, single mom, dog lover and appreciates a good sense of humor. She is the Founder & CEO of The Be Influence and Owner of Proforma Specialty Marketing, a multiple six figure printing and promotional products company, both in Dallas, Texas. www.thebeinfluence.com

Below are the various ways that you can connect with Pam and learn more about what she has to offer.

Website:
www.thebeinfluence.com

Twitter:
www.twitter.com/thebeinfluence

Facebook:
www.facebook.com/thebeinfluence

MARSHA SHERRILL
Speaker, Coach, Consultant & Author

Tell us a little about yourself. We want to learn about the person behind the brand.

I was born and raised in California. The San Francisco Bay Area to be more specific, but have lived in the southern region (Los Angeles and San Diego areas) as well. I am the second oldest of six children and the oldest daughter. As a child I had a stuttering problem, I believe this is one of the main reasons I took to reading and writing. At the age of 11 my grandmother gave me my first diary and I started writing and still write, in now what I call a journal.

As a young girl I cared deeply for others. Maybe I was co-dependent. I especially cared for under-dogs, those who lacked confidence, the needy and the targets for bullies. I would stand up for them, which led to being involved in physical altercations. I would speak out on injustices which all led to suspensions and even an expulsion. I truly disliked confrontation and conflict, but I would not run from it either.

I moved to Texas in 2003, which has proved to be the one of the best things to ever happen to me! I have been on the most exciting, joy-filled, scary adventure ever since. This has been my first experience living outside California as an adult. It feels like I get to make up life every day. I get to choose whether it's a good day and what my attitude is going to be. Every day there is something new. I could decide what my day was going to be like when I lived in California, but an experience I had when I first got here changed my perspective.

My very first night in Texas was filled with wonderment mixed with fear of the unknown. I slept very well and woke up refreshed and excited about my day. It was a Saturday and I wanted to find a few essential businesses; gas station, grocery store, drug store, nail salon, shopping areas and beauty salon. I showered and got dressed for the day. The sun was out and the sky was clear and a beautiful blue. I put on a light jacket and opened the apartment door, and then I froze. The realization that I had no idea where I was going, no idea where anything was located, do I turn left or right when I drive out of the garage? I knew absolutely nothing about the area.

I was overwhelmed with fear. I stood there at the threshold that separates the hallway and my apartment. I slowly backed inside the apartment and started to cry. I took out my journal and started to write about my fears and anxieties. Through my writing I came to the conclusion that I was going to make this an adventure, everything is brand new. There is no right or wrong. I will just make it all up as I go. I still hold to that principle today. I take the "scenic routes" quite a bit, intentional or not, and have accepted that as part of my adventure. Because I know this about myself, I leave in plenty of time to recoup and correct and still reach my destination on time. I love living here and am deeply grateful for the person and the opportunity that brought me here.

As an avid reader, I could spend hours in a bookstore. Reading is an adventure in itself. I enjoy writing, meeting people and socializing. I am "single again" (I prefer that phrase over "divorced"), no children, love my church family and all my friends, many of whom are like family.

I was in customer service, sales and operations for two major media companies for over 30 years. I have led successful sales divisions for many years, but the best part of my job experience was developing skills of the people who reported up to me. Coaching, honing and sharpening skills, and helping people realize their highest potential were fulfilling to me. That compassionate spirit for helping others is a part of who I am which is why I started my coaching, speaking and consulting business. I want people to succeed, to be the best they can be on the job and in their personal life.

I left corporate America in 2008 which, unbeknownst to me, was the end of a life chapter and the genesis of my next chapter of life.

Share with us what your business is and why you wanted to start this business.

Over the years I knew many people who desired to start their own businesses and to be entrepreneurs. It was never a desire or even thought of mine. It seemed like too much work, instability and uncertainty. Besides, what could I do that people would buy from me? What could I invent?

I had been looking for another position in corporate. I was applying for management positions at several companies, large and small. I had never felt so rejected in my life. I came very close to being hired by three prestigious companies, but at the last minute there was a shift. The rejections devastated me.

One company decided to hire from within (which they told me was their practice, but they really liked me). The other decided to change the job from director to trainer. I found out later that one of the executives there had a child graduating college... well, you get the picture. The third and largest company was so excited I was interested in coming on board.

We talked quite a bit. He was the VP of Human Resources. He asked if I had a resume. He looked it over carefully and quietly. Once he discovered my previous salary he tried to hand me back my resume saying they could not afford me. I did not want to take the resume back. I could not believe this was happening! His thinking is that once I find a company who would pay close to what I was accustomed to, I would leave his company and they could not afford to take that chance. Much later, like months later, I had to concede that he was probably right. In all cases, I was willing to take a 6-figure cut in pay just to be able to work. This was my breaking point.

I was beyond devastated. I no longer felt needed, worthy, valued, relevant or wanted.

- When did you know you were meant to launch your own business?

One evening while perusing the internet, actually Facebook, I noticed an ad with the words "Breakthrough", "seeking purpose in your life?" It sparked my curiosity. There was a number to call to set up a free consultation. I called and set up an appointment. I was so excited on the day of the phone appointment. I was feeling hopeful for the first time in a while. The lady who came on the line was so loving, compassionate and caring and seemed truly interested in me. We talked for nearly an hour. There were tears as I spoke of what I called my dilemma. Allyson told me that she could help me break through to finding my life purpose and break free from the traps of a limiting mindset. At the end of our conversation she prayed. I was so touched.

Allyson worked with me through the breakthrough processes. There were some things that came up for me that were very emotional and freeing all at the same time. I experienced revelations about how I felt about myself, how I lived a self-limiting lifestyle, yet I looked good on the outside. My internal and external did not match. My whole mindset about me and where I fit in the world needed an overhaul. A major overhaul was in order. There had to be a shift in my thinking.

Part of my limiting belief was, setting aside my skills and abilities; if people found out about my background they would not hire me. So, if I were to get a lower paying job I could stay in corporate and hide among the masses.

You see, I am a recovering alcoholic and addict. At the time I had nearly 20 years in recovery. Even with that amount of time clean and sober people still frown. If I started my own business as a consultant people are more apt to find out the truth about me. Little did I know that my background, my previous lifestyle would become the foundation of my business. My beliefs may have held some truth, but the bigger truth is that people needed to hear my story and have hope for their future.

Through many conversations, some very casual, I found so many people who seemed lost, but had settled into their life. They seemed to do things by habit rather than desire. Their thoughts were "this is as good as it's going to get". Several people, mainly women who had left their jobs either by retirement, layoff or voluntary departure, raised their kids, or were still on the job but felt less than fulfilled. They felt the same way I did, that my best life was behind me and now I am on the decline.

I truly felt I was all used up. My youth was gone. Going through several deep self-discovery processes with my coach coupled with talking to other people, I began to realize that was something more to life. I had a purpose. I was not used up! I began my pursuit of purpose. It was such an exciting time. The evolution of Marsha (which later became a blog). I felt hopeful. Pursuing purpose is not an overnight discovery. I was open and willing to do the work to discover my purpose.

Ideas and possibilities began to form. I would question or dismiss each one for one reason or another. One of my coaches, Stella, would ask "why not you?" or tell me "just do it!" She recommended books that opened my eyes to even more possibilities. I was in the midst of a mindset shift thanks to a lot of prayer, spiritual mentors and caring, compassionate coaches.

The first step toward identifying and clarifying my life purpose was to become willing to allow the change in my perspective. I had to be willing to work hard for it, no matter how difficult the process. I had to be willing to dig deep into my person and undo some of the improper ways of thinking that had been ingrained in me over the years. I needed detoxification.

What has being in business for yourself done for you?

Being in business as an entrepreneur has built my confidence in many ways. Being an entrepreneur has shown me that fear is an emotion and I can walk through it with knees knocking, tears flowing, and doubt looming. It is temporary. I had to press through no matter what I was feeling. I am stronger, smarter and more creative than I ever thought I was or could be.

I have realized that all my life experiences, the ups and downs, the sunny days, the dark times brought me to a time such as this. Everything that has happened to me adds up to now! There are people that need to hear how I survived, how I got over. I still have the same compassion and desire to help others. It is my mission, my purpose for being on earth.

My life is not over just because I parted ways with corporate America. My best life is not behind me, it is in front of me. Everything in my past was my purpose at that time and it was a learning ground for what was to come. I am vibrant, needed and relevant. It is time to act like it. I had to do the work for my comeuppance.

If someone asked you, who are your ideal clients, what would you say?

As far as coaching, my ideal client are women who have raised the kids who are now grown and left home, empty nesters, women who left their jobs either by retiring, downsizing or a voluntary departure. She could be a woman who is suddenly single-again or just seeking more from life. My ideal client feels she may be withering away, but something inherent is tugging at her, telling her to get up and do something.

These women may not feel they have anything to offer the world. They use to have dreams, but can't quite remember what they were. They may lack the confidence to acknowledge how they are feeling and to act upon them. Maybe she knows what her passions and dreams are but fear is telling her they are silly to try to start something at this stage of life. All of these are self-limiting beliefs.

These women are in need of a breakthrough, they need a shift in their thinking. A rebirthing, a revival, a renewal!

As a speaker, I speak at conferences that empower women in areas of health and wellness, spirituality and well-being. My range of focus includes topics such as reviving dreams, discovering passions, pursuit of purpose, visioning the future, designing the life they desire as well as offering hope for a greater future.

As a consultant, my ideal clientele would be businesses who employ frontline supervisors or employees who have are being prepared and groomed for future leadership roles. These clients are skilled and have the desire to grow in the business, but may need extra guidance, mentoring and coaching to develop and build on their skills. I work with managers to get an understanding of their expectations and training areas needing to be covered with the employee.

How do you measure success and what is your definition of success?

Success can be measured in many ways. I love when the people I have worked with get clear about what they want to do with their lives; when they are more confident to make decisions and choices for building their future. They have hope in their lives. They start to talk differently. They show up in the world differently. They realize they are someone who has a purpose and can and will live with intention and authenticity.

It is so satisfying to see a woman live with a purpose and boldness after putting the tools they learned to practice. They have experienced a paradigm shift in how they view themselves. It is a heartfelt feeling to know someone's life has been changed for the better with some help from me. When I see my clients shine with this type of inner-peace, I call it success.

In the consulting world, success can be measured by the person's performance, productivity or exceeding goals set mutually between the manager and student. During discussions I deem success in follow up sessions with the student and hearing how they are beginning to excel in areas where they were once challenged.

Another way I view success is when someone shows up for a conference call, buys a product, signs up for a session, hires me as a consultant or coach, invites me to speak, completing an assessment, launching a new program, coming up with a new idea, letting my creativity run free without judgment, or completing a new program or module.

All success does not have to be grandiose. There are smaller but very relevant successes along the way that make up the large successes. Some successes are not seen by everyone. Overnight successes do not exist. There were many little successes that brought successful people to the top of their success mountain.

I also see success as getting up and back into the game after a so-called "failure". Failure is one of the best teachers if we know how to use it. Learn from it. Apply what you have learned and keep trying, keep working, keep pressing on. You will eventually reap what you have sown.

What was the biggest obstacle you've encountered since being in business? How did you overcome it?

One of the biggest obstacles in starting and running my own business was fear of investing in myself. I feared the cost of investing. In the beginning I could not reconcile the amount spent with the amount of income. My view of investing in my learning or coaching was on the money going out and not the return on investment. Once again, it was a mindset that needed desperately to be changed. On occasion I will revert to that old way of thinking. Today, I can gladly say that I recognize it and work to develop ways to leverage the expense.

It can be fearful, especially when the "what-ifs' would show up. What if this coach doesn't deliver? What if I fail? What if? What if? What if?

One of the tools I have learned is to turn the question around. What if the coach is awesome and delivers what they said they would? What if I succeed? What if the tools I have learned really do work?

Then there's that word "failure". I had to look at it differently. If I learn the lesson and apply what I learn, is it still considered a failure? What if I made failure a friend rather than a foe? The answers to these questions deplete the negative mindset of power over me. I am once again motivated, inspired and determined to reach my life goals.

One of my mantras: "the only failure there is would be for me to quit".

What have you learned about yourself in running your business?

I enjoy working for myself. It is very hard work. There are parts of the work I love to do and other responsibilities I dislike, but it is my duty to get those things as well. It is of utmost importance to get really clear and acknowledge that I do not have all the answers. I cannot build this business or reach my goals alone. That saying "no (wo) man in an island" is real. I need help such as a coach, mentor, an assistant and people to fill roles that will help grow my business. I need support groups and networking groups. I do not have to know everything about everything. What a relief.

Procrastination and perfectionism are enemies of a business owner. Once I acknowledged my level of procrastination and that it is not my friend, I had to work to eliminate procrastination from my life. Many times I would find myself in a self-imposed bind because I set something aside. Sometimes I would forget to do some things because of putting it off until later. I still get tempted but I tools to recognize and combat it!

If someone would have told me that I was a perfectionist, I would have argued with them down to the ground. Not me! What a rude awakening I had. In starting my business I would try to get everything perfect before I would launch my business. Then it was trying to get every program perfect. There was nearly a year delay in launching a program because I wanted everything in place. I needed everything perfect. Guess what? What a relief to know it is never perfect. There will be refining, making better, deleting programs that are no longer relevant, starting new programs. We change, the needs of our clients may change and we have to stay flexible to answer the call of change.

Self-work and staying on top of my industry is not something that is learned once. It is constant. Bettering myself, checking my mindset, making adjustments in my thinking, showing up at all times with an open heart, giving more of myself, being intentional and authentic is a daily exercise. I am constantly taking my pulse, not to see if I am alive, but to make sure I am on track. I must honor myself throughout this entire process.

What was your most rewarding experience since starting your own business?

One experience that stands out for me is the client who I could not tell if she was paying attention or understood what I was saying. I did not know if I was reaching her. She was always quiet so I did not know where she was emotionally, mentally, spiritually or if she was getting what I was teaching (this was in a group coaching session).

I was truly surprised each time she turned in her assignments. One day she and I had an opportunity to talk privately. She asked me a few questions. They were deep and thoughtful questions too. After answering and giving her some insight we began to chat about general things in life. At the end of the conversation we were about to hang up she said:

"Marsha, thank you so much, you are bringing out things in me I did not know existed, you have inspired me to be more, to reach for the prize. I have a purpose in life that I didn't know I had. You are a God-send. I appreciate you so much!"

Wow! I got choked up trying to thank her. After hanging up I thanked God for her and her kind words. It goes to show, that what I think I see may not be what is really going on. In this case, what I thought I saw was not the truth. I was making a difference. What a lesson for me.

What 3 things do you now wish you would have known when you started?

I now know I could have launched my business and programs a couple of years sooner. There is no perfect time. I wish I knew for certain that I have what it takes to make a difference in the lives of people hurting and in the world and who feel there is no hope. I know that investing in myself is crucial. I cannot be student and teacher for myself. I do not know everything about everything!

How do you keep yourself motivated and encouraged when things don't go right?

To keep myself motivated and encouraged I have accountability partners who keep me on track and help keep the "crazies" away. I have friends that I have met at events or conferences that are in the same field or are entrepreneurs. They love to eat, drink coffee, talk and laugh. We get together and talk about what is going on in our businesses, successes, challenges, solutions and new applications.

Soon I am motivated and inspired to be brave and take bigger risks, start new programs, check my rating system. My mind is a whirlwind of new and bigger ideas. My accountability partners are the same way. We laugh, cry, share stories, books, give wisdom and great hugs!

There are times too, though, that I need to encourage myself. When I do not feel like talking, or eating, or putting on clothes for that matter. I know it is time for me to get deeper into my spiritual practices (prayer and meditation); I will peruse my bookshelves looking for specific topics or just to scan a book.

I will do the same with my Bible. I may write what I am feeling or write whatever comes to mind. I am a cloud watcher. I love to watch the sizes and shapes of clouds. That brings me peace. During these times, I am gentle with myself as I realize it is time for me to be still.

What's your biggest business goal over the next 12 months and what will you do to meet it?

One of my biggest goals is to have my own personal book completed and published. I know I need help in organizing my thoughts. I am working with an editor and copywriter. I want my book to be positive and uplifting with practical applications. Having a regular schedule, on the calendar to work on the book is a must. There will be deadlines and meetings scheduled with those assisting me on the project. Included in the schedule is a list of all the tasks that are required in publishing a book. This will be my blueprint and roadmap to help me hire all the necessary people in all the required roles and to stay on track.

What advice would you give to a woman entrepreneur who is ready to take her business to the next level?

Make sure you have the right coach to help you move forward. Realize you are not alone and cannot accomplish your goals and start your business on your own. You will need help. You need a support group. Surround yourself with people you admire and who are going in the same direction you are.

Get rid of naysayers and people who question you or try to discourage you. Trust the process, it takes time. Be gentle with yourself. Do not compare yourself to others. You may be comparing your beginning with someone's middle. Keep going no matter what. If you feel discouraged, talk to someone, we've all been there. Pray, meditate, pray again.

Network. Continue to invest in yourself. It will never be a perfect ~ START.

One of the biggest struggles women entrepreneurs have is how to price themselves. What advice would you share about pricing your services and offerings?

There are still times I struggle with setting my rates based on my value. There is value in being brave enough to see my value. She said to me "those who cannot afford your rates are not your clients'. Simple as that! When she told me that, there was nothing more for me to say. I must value myself before I can expect anyone else to.

What must have resources would you recommend to use in your business?

The resources I recommend, that I cannot be without are:

- ✓ A visionary coach
- ✓ Network group. Choose the group that is actually helping you learn about business, not just sell to each other.
- ✓ Accountability partner(s)
- ✓ On-line staffing platforms i.e.: Elance, Fiverr, Odesk. There is a myriad of such businesses or individuals)
- ✓ Virtual assistant

- ✓ Research books (continuous learning about your field, if appropriate)
- ✓ Mastermind programs

What makes you a Woman That Impacts? How are you impacting your world?

I am a woman that impacts the world because I desire to make a difference sharing my life experiences combined with learned knowledge. I bring hope where there is none. I live to bring clarity where there is confusion or unknowing. Another mantra: "As long as we have breath we have a purpose."

We can discover our dreams. We can manifest the dream. We can live with intention. We can live the life we desire. It is never too late. Never!

I am here to help all my sisters shine.

My tagline is: Envision, Embrace, Ignite

Continue the Conversation with Marsha Sherrill:

Marsha Sherrill is a dynamic life purpose coach, speaker, leadership development coach and author. Her studies and life experiences enable her to intuitively help others succeed. She believes that as long as you have breath, you can breakthrough to live a life of purpose and excellence!

Marsha has been driven to encourage women to envision, embrace and ignite dreams and aspirations. She inspires women to live life with intention, authenticity, passion, power and purpose.

Below are the various ways that you can connect with Marsha and learn more about what she has to offer.

Website:
www.marshasherrill.com

Twitter:
www.twitter.com/marshas

Facebook:
www.facebook.com/marshasherrillcoach

DARLENE TEMPLETON
Founder, Templeton & Associates

Tell us a little about yourself. We want to learn about the woman behind the brand.

I was born in Fort Worth, Texas as the third child in a family that would total 4. My father was an entrepreneur with an 8th grade education and was an amazing leader. He took a service station in Fort Worth and turned it into a service/gas station, state inspection provider, boat dealership, and the first U-Haul dealer in Fort Worth. My father was charismatic. People loved him and he could work any room in a matter of minutes. People in the area still remember my father.

My mother worked alongside my father in the service station. She knew more about cars than many men in the area – back in the 50s especially, this was a very progressive position for a woman. My father told her once she needed to wear a skirt to work and, being strong-willed herself, she told him she would not work at the service station unless she could wear pants. He never mentioned it again.

As my mother was working at the service station, my crib was right in the middle of everything. I spent my toddler years there, interacting with employees and customers. They talked to me, picked me up, and I never met a stranger. I grew up in that service station and watched my father build his business. I am certain I get my leadership passion and talent from him.

I have always been strong-willed. One of my favorite stories from my childhood is that when I went to daycare, I refused to eat the oatmeal served by the school. I insisted on bringing my own Cheerios. Some would say nothing has changed in that regard!

My father died when I was 9 years old and it completely changed my life. My older siblings were both married and out of the house by this point, so I was the oldest kid and wound up in charge. I watched my mom struggle after my dad died and I made a promise to myself that I would never be in a place where I did not have some means to make a living.

I had already been the "go to" person in most areas of my life and after Daddy died, that just became more pronounced. I have always been the person people go to get things done, to get people together.

In 1963, a few years after Daddy died, Mom moved us to San Francisco. Remember the Civil Rights movement was going strong in the 1960s and I moved from Fort Worth, Texas, to the inner city in San Francisco. It was quite a cultural difference, but I ate it up. I spent sixth and seventh grade in San Francisco and kept up my normal routine of excelling in school and functioning as a go-between for various groups. I was friends with kids in the popular group, kids in the smart group, and so on. I enjoyed people, was involved in student government, and often bridged the gaps among groups to the advantage of everyone. We moved back to Texas the summer before 9th grade. I became president of the student body and was so excited.

I was always an overachiever. I worked really hard, earned good grades in school, scored very high on the SAT, was salutatorian of my graduating class, and won a full scholarship to any Texas college I wanted to attend. The only reason I was the salutatorian was that I had earned a B in my citizenship class, what a surprise! I took vocational classes and excelled there as well. I was able to take shorthand at 145 words per minute and I typed at 125 words per minute. This was a big deal in the 1970s.

I had a Vocational Office Education (VOE) teacher who made a huge difference in my life. Mrs. Watts taught me how to be a professional. She showed confidence in me and really served as a cheerleader in my life. I had several supportive teachers, but there was something about Mrs. Watts that stood out as a game changer for me. I still keep in touch with her, and in fact have delivered several talks to groups at her request. She's always told me she's proud of me and I can't emphasize enough that if it weren't for Mrs. Watts and her support, I wouldn't be where I am now.

I said as much in the first speech she asked me to deliver at a VOE teachers' in-service several years after I had been at IBM for a few years. I spoke about leadership, how important it is to be a role model, a team member, and a leader. I told the group how Mrs. Watts had taught me to hone my skills and use my strengths. She is an amazing woman and I still use the lessons she taught me so long ago today. I teach what she taught, plus my own twist on ramping it up.

Mrs. Watts always looked so put-together, so professionally dressed and professionally coiffed that when a group of us saw her at an outdoor school function in jeans, we swore it could not be her! She told us simply, "I'm human, too, you know. I have children and I have a life outside of this program." Looking back, seeing her as a whole person made a positive impact on me.

Writing this about Mrs. Watts has reminded me it is time to reach out to her again as it's been several months since we have spoken. I cannot wait to catch up with her again!

Rather than go to college, I turned down the scholarship I earned and married my high school sweetheart at 18 years old. This did not please anyone, especially Mrs. Watts. She wanted me to use that scholarship and follow the pattern I had set in excelling in school and achieving my goals Instead, I went to O29 Key Punch School the month after graduation and got married 4 months later.

I went through a personnel agency to apply for a secretarial position with Texas Electric. When I showed up for my first interview, I knew I was in trouble because I could see I was younger than the hiring manager's youngest child. He told me I had great skills, but no experience, so did not want to hire me. I asked him, "Mr. Bleck, if no one will hire me, how will I ever get any experience?" He told me I had a great point and the personnel agency called me the next day to tell me I had gotten the job. I worked for Mr. Bleck for 2 years and still keep in touch with him, too.

I was working as a secretary for Texas Electric in Fort Worth and my husband's business was doing well, so I decided to go to school to earn my teaching degree. I gave three months' notice at Texas Electric and made plans. After I stopped working, I was preparing to register for classes when my husband came home from work one day and told me he did not want to be married anymore. He told me I needed to move out.

I was 22, unemployed, soon to be unmarried, and soon to be without a place to live. To say I freaked out a bit would be an understatement. I remembered the vow I made to myself after Daddy died never to be stuck without a means to make a living, so I applied for several jobs. One of the jobs I applied for was a sales position with a women's clothing company. I was one of 50 applicants and made it all the way to the final round as one of two finalists. I went in for the last meeting, fully expecting to be offered the job. The hiring manager told me I was the most qualified for the position, but that I was too unstable given my pending divorce, so he would not hire me. Of course, someone could not even say that now, but in 1974, this was not uncommon.

I was devastated and left in tears. Even in my despair, I could hear my mother's voice in my head, saying, "Just do it, honey. You know what you need to do, so just get it done." This was well before the now well-known slogan employed by Nike to "Just Do It." If only Mother had given them the idea, she could be worth millions! Shortly thereafter, I was driving through town on an errand, dressed in jeans and a t-shirt. I passed an IBM building and decided, on a whim, to stop by and pick up an application.

As soon as I opened the door, I knew I had made a mistake. Everyone in the building was in suits – remember this was 1974. I held my head high and asked for an application to take home and fill out. The woman who handed me the application told me to fill it out then and there. I was so self-conscious and embarrassed about my clothing, but I filled out the application and tried to leave. The woman reads over my application and asked if I could stay a few minutes to talk with her. I said yes, though I could feel everyone's eyes boring through me, wondering what this ragamuffin was doing in the offices of IBM dressed as I was. She asked me to come in for an interview the next day.

I borrowed a suit from a friend who worked for a nearby legal firm because I had neither a suit nor the money to buy one in time for the interview.

I interviewed for and was offered a position called a supplemental secretary on a 90-day probation. This meant they would re-evaluate my skills and my fit with the company at 90 days and decide whether to offer me a full-time position.

On day 45, they decided I was the right fit and decided to hire me right then, instead of waiting the traditional 90 days. I was hired into a brand new division of IBM as a secretary. Over the years, I moved up to a manager position, a second line manager position, and so on. I ran huge projects and dealt with top-tier clients with globally recognized brand names.

IBM moved me from Fort Worth to Dallas to El Paso, where I was the Business Operations Manager for our sales organization. The Maquiladora Program was just starting along the US/Mexico border and many of our largest clients had plants on both sides of the border. That became my project and we created a program for our largest clients to do business internationally. I worked with IBM Latin America to develop and implement this program worldwide. This program included Ford, A. C. Nielson, Sony,

Hitachi, Mitsubishi, and many other top-tier clients in IBM. This was the basis for the IBM international marketing program that I later deployed worldwide. .

I went to work for IBM Latin America and I was the first woman to serve as the Operations Manager for all of Brazil, and all of Mexico. These were the two largest organizations in IBM Latin America and I was always the only woman in this position. This was an interesting and exciting time in my career.

I had high standards for my team members as well as for myself. During my early years as a manager, my team nicknamed me "Redline" because I would always use a red pen or pencil to make edits to their work. They would say, "Oh, there she goes, redlining us again!"

IBM moved me to New York in 1990, where I thought I would probably stay and retire. I was deploying the Maquiladora Program for Latin America. Of course I did not stay there, and in 1993, IBM promoted and moved me to Boca Raton, Florida. I spent two years there, where I managed the supply chain and manufacturing for the IBM Latin America PC company. In 1995, I went to Raleigh as part of the Microsoft project for all IBM PCs out of Raleigh. I was the PC Operations Manager, focused on customer relationship management. We built the metrics and measurement systems that were adopted across the entire company. I spent many years in process work.

One day in Raleigh, I met a man and told a girlfriend the next day that I was going to marry him. She thought I was crazy; I had been single for 18 years and hadn't seen a need to change that. Sure enough, I married that man 17 years ago. We have two grown sons, two incredible daughters-in-law, and four amazing grandchildren. I finally got the family I had always wanted; it just took a different route than I thought it would.

In the early 2000s, I got into business consulting with the sales organization. I worked with business partners – again, globally recognized customer names – to determine how they wanted to work with IBM. Eventually, I said I wanted out of management, but remained in business consulting.

I never did go to college. I like to say I earned my PHD from IBM. I succeeded at IBM because I held close the values of Perseverance, Hard work, and Determination.

Share with us what your business is and why you wanted to start this business.

In 2003, IBM sent me to a class with Coaches Training Institute (CTI), the largest coaching organization in the world. I knew without a doubt on the first day that this was the name for what I had spent my life doing. I was a coach! I had always helped people, I had always wanted to see people achieve their goals and I had always felt it my duty to help however I could. Having a name for it made all the difference for me. It struck me that it was my calling, my purpose, to empower and coach others. I just knew this was exactly what I was meant to do.

I knew when I retired from IBM that I would be a coach, so I started putting a plan together. I retired from IBM after 36 years and Templeton & Associates was born soon after.

When did you know you were meant to launch your own business?

It was during that first session with CTI that it hit me. I told a dear friend who was with me that day that this was what I was meant to do.

What has being in business for yourself done for you?

I have met so many amazing people along this journey, above and beyond what I could have asked for if I had known to ask for it. Meeting new people, different people from different backgrounds, has really helped me build a community. It has helped me grow in my ability to be in service to others, and it has given me an amazing support system and become the leader that I am today.

People I have met along the way have become clients, advisors, mentors, and friends. I know without a doubt that I can pick up the phone at any time and call any one of several people who will do anything they can to help with whatever I need. It has given me personal satisfaction to know I am living on purpose and living my mission. I was born to do this work and I am so thankful to be doing it now. I have always been the confidante, the empowerer, the leader, and now I get to focus specifically on those things!

Living on purpose, to me, means I am doing what I was intended to do. I am helping people, I am in service to those who need me, and I am helping others live their mission and their purpose. Nothing gives me greater satisfaction than when one of my clients sees success.

If someone asked who your ideal clients are, what would you say?

I serve men and women looking to take that next step, whether personally, professionally, or both. My clients are people and organizations who want to up their leadership game.

One of my clients said that I serve as her mirror. I help her see what others see, what she can't because she is looking out from the inside. I help my clients come up with strategies and plans to establish and then meet or exceed their goals. As an objective outside observer, I can see things that someone "on the inside" cannot see. I do not tell my clients what to do; I simply help them see the answers that have been waiting inside them all along.

How do you measure success and what is your definition of success?

My success is inextricably tied to the success of my clients and their achievements. My definition of success is to be doing the things we are passionate about, things we are happy about, and whatever puts us in service to others.

What's the biggest obstacle you've encountered since being in business? How did you overcome it?

My biggest obstacle has always been myself! I have not overcome myself, but I have learned when to listen to that critical voice in my head and when to ignore the nasty things she says about me. Despite my strong skills, I still felt like I had to work twice as hard as a woman in a male-dominated field and company, as progressive as IBM was. As a person without a degree, I find myself in situations where people are introducing themselves and they are using words like "Harvard," "Yale," and other prestigious educational institutions and this leads to feelings of inadequacy.

I was so afraid of failing that I would overwork myself. The simplest word that describes how I have always operated is "overachiever." It has taken me many years to realize that I learn by failing. I have had to give myself permission to try, to fail, to learn, and to grow. I have finally come to realize that good enough is good enough, and that "perfect" is the enemy of "great."

What have you learned about yourself in running your business?

I love having my own business. I am really good at what I am good at and I enjoy it immensely. I have learned what I am not good at and I have learned to ask for help with those things. I used to cry during tax time, trying to do everything myself. I finally hired my incredible bookkeeper and it has been the single biggest professional relief for me. I talk to my clients about being the face of their business, that they are the only ones who can sell their business, but there are other people out there to fill in the holes on things they do not enjoy or excel in.

What was your most rewarding experience since starting your own business?

The whole experience has been so incredible that I really struggle with this question. My most rewarding days are when a client is able to make the changes necessary to live her or his purpose. Each client's goals are so different and specific and it is really exciting to have front row seats to their success.

I have really enjoyed my volunteer work with Dress for Success' professional program, the Going Places Network. The women in that program are really growing and finding themselves and it is such a treat to be part of their journey.

What 3 things do you wish you'd known when you started?

- Trust your gut instincts because they are always right. Always, always, every time, without fail.
- Create an "advisory board" of people you can go to for support with a variety of needs. My support network keeps me going on days when I struggle.
- Learning to say no is imperative in any business, but especially when in business for yourself. I have learned that when I say yes to something, I am saying no to something else, so it is best to be very specific about how I choose to spend my time and energy.

How do you keep yourself motivated and encouraged when things don't go right?

I have an amazing support system, which serves not only as my advisory board, but also as dear friends. They help and support me in every way. I also work with two coaches who keep me on track. The most important thing I do is remember to celebrate the things that have gone right instead of wallowing in the things that are not going the way I think they should.

I am also finally trusting my gut; I call it my "foo-foos," in all areas of my life.

What's your biggest business goal over the next 12 months and what will you do to meet it?

I want to continue to grow my business in three areas: speaking, coaching and consulting, and the GR8 Women Leaders program I joined in 2014 and I am so excited about its growth and where we are going in 2015. The women in this program are amazing and are truly taking their lives to the next level.

I know that I need what I call maniacal focus – to keep on track and not allow myself to be distracted. I may be practicing saying no a lot more in the next year than I have before.

What advice would you give to a woman entrepreneur who is ready to take her business to the next level?

Find your passion, enlist the help of your support team, and remember the answer is always no until you ask.

One of the biggest struggles women entrepreneurs have is how to price their services/business. What advice would you share about pricing your services and offerings?

For a long time, I gave away so much because I had not realized my own value yet. I was undercharging. I had a client come to me after she had tried working with another coach without success. When she told me what she had been paying this other coach, I was shocked and realized I was seriously undervaluing myself.

You must value yourself first so that others will see it. Talk with others in your field, talk with potential clients to find out what they are willing to, or are paying. A good rule of thumb is that if people accept your prices with no discussion, you are probably not charging enough. If people refuse to do business with you, you are charging too much. If people push back a bit, but negotiate, you are probably charging the right prices. People are willing to pay good money for your services and offerings; don't sell yourself short!

Also, keep in mind that when we undercut each other's prices, we are simply racing to the bottom. We are devaluing ourselves and our industry, as well as small business in general.

What must-have resources would you recommend to use in your business?

This is a different answer for everyone, but the most important pieces for me are:

- Have an advisory board, a trusted set of friends, partners, colleagues, and mentors, whatever that you can brainstorm with, depend on, and who can, help keep you on track.
- Having a bookkeeper/CPA has saved my business and my sanity!

- My virtual assistant helps me keep the details under control so I don't get overwhelmed in the weeds and can focus on what I enjoy most.

What makes you a Woman That Impacts? How are you impacting your world?

I am a leadership expert, I am passionate, I love helping people, and I am committed to helping people grow, especially women, and be in service. My experience has given me the tools to have a huge impact in many areas. I can now comfortably claim expertise in the areas of engagement, empowerment, and inspiration.

My story all boils down to the fact that I was born with this purpose and I am so thankful to be able to live my calling and help others.

Continue the Conversation with Darlene Templeton:

Darlene is the CEO of Templeton & Associates. She is a professional speaker, certified executive coach, business consultant, trainer and author. Darlene specializes in leadership and transformation for corporations and professionals, specifically for those who want to make a greater impact personally and professionally. She held multiple management and leadership positions during her career at IBM and brings her 36 years of experience, to her work and her clients, and provides a level of mastery that is extraordinary.

Below are the various ways that you can connect with Darlene and learn more about what she has to offer.

Website:
www.darlenetempleton.com

Twitter:
www.twitter.com/darlenetemple

Facebook:
www.facebook.com/darlene.templeton.58

ROSE MCGRANE-COLAROSSI

Co-Owner, The Egg & Restaurants located in Addison/N. Dallas, W. Plano/Carrollton, Denton

If you had asked me as a child, or even as a young adult, if I would have ever imagined myself living outside of Dallas, Texas, let alone owning several restaurants – I would have thought you were crazy.

Hello! My name is Rose McGrane-Colarossi. I am the former 10+ years owner of a Curves 30-minute workout facility located in Flower Mound, Texas and the current co-owner of **The Egg & Restaurants** located in **Addison/N. Dallas, W. Plano/Carrollton, Denton** with my husband and our oldest son as managing partner. www.TheEggandIrestaurants.com. Facebook: The Egg and I – Addison/N. Dallas, W. Plano/Carrollton, Denton.

Tell us a little about yourself. We want to learn about the person behind the brand.

I was born in the Bronx, New York, and raised in Yorktown Heights, New York a suburb about 1 hour north of New York City. I am the oldest of four children. My younger brother and sister (twins) and I were raised by my mother Rosemarie Joyce, the youngest daughter of Irish immigrants. My early childhood memories are of me being surrounded by our extended family and having great times running and playing on the sidewalks of the Bronx. We attended Catholic School and I walked to church on Sunday with my Irish Grandmother who would talk lovingly to me with her Irish brogue about her childhood in Ireland. When I was 10 years-old my mother remarried a New York City Fireman who had grown up with one of my aunts, and we moved to Yorktown Heights, New York. I continued to attend Catholic school throughout elementary and high school.

After graduating high school, my boyfriend's mother, a wonderful woman from England, insisted that I interview for the receptionist position at her husband's company so that I would have a good job while attending college. She had come to the United States as a nanny and knew what it was like for a young girl needing to support herself. I worked hard and was a quick study. I started gravitating toward the marketing department and soon secured a position working for the VP of Marketing. I later secured a job as the assistant to the VP of Marketing at a major consumers goods company.

I attended the University of Connecticut while working to pursue a career in Child Psychology. A Psychology Professor of mine introduced me to the Autistic community through a work-study program. I fell in love with the first child and family I met. They wanted me and a fellow student/friend to work with their son and arranged to have us trained by one of the best behavior modification therapy programs in the country. I absolutely loved it!

I met my husband of 23 years while at a work event geared for children. His son and daughter and my youngest brother (my mother started the trend of having a child at age 43) became friends after seeing one another at several of the events. After dating for four years, we married and went on to have two more children and adopted a rescue dog named Rusty. I love children and I love dogs. I also like to read and I belong to a book club. I like to hike, power walk, travel, stand up paddleboard, and garden. I really have a thing for furniture and my house has an eclectic mix of findings with a story behind each piece. Other than the Amalfi Coast in Italy, my favorite place in the world is on any a white sandy beach with sea blue water.

What you have learned about yourself running your business?

First and foremost, I am a people person. I love to talk to people whether it is one-on-one, in a group, as a speaker, on television or radio promoting our restaurants, at networking meetings - you name it. I have never met a stranger, and I am very comfortable in all scenarios. People simply fascinate me. I do not understand getting into an elevator and not saying hello to someone. I do not believe in passing people on the street and not smiling and saying, "Hello." I inherited that quality from my mother. My mother also passed on the counselor gene. You see, no matter where I go, people tell me their life story. I feel honored and do not take what people share with me lightly. I also think that being kind to one another should be first-nature.

In 1997 my husband was offered a position within his company located in Dallas, Texas. Although the thought of living far away from my family did not appeal to me, the cost of living was much lower than Connecticut. We had two children quickly approaching the college years, a toddler, and one on the way - so we took the offer.

Share with us what your business is and why you wanted to start this business.

After a year or two, I started to research careers that would allow me to be home before and after school for my children. One day my car literally turned into a retail center and I looked up and there was a sign that said Curves on it. Something told me to go inside. Long story made short, the manager of this 30-minute fitness center for women convinced me to try working out there for a week free.

During my first workout, I could completely see myself owning a Curves. True story... Two nights later my mother called me from New York and told me that she had driven into a retail center and found this incredible concept that she thought would be perfect for me to open in Texas. It was called... you guessed it... Curves! My husband's jaw dropped open and he and I knew it was meant to be!

Eight months later and after much research, I signed a franchise agreement to open a club in Flower Mound, Texas. I hired a contractor and worked out the design aspects of my club based on my visiting over 20 different Curves locations. I literally rigged a piece of chalk to a stick and drew on the floor exactly where I wanted everything to go in real-life size. The contractor loved it. I took all my prior marketing experience and started advertising for our grand opening. It was very exciting. I had also made friends with a woman at the Curves Owners' meeting who opened a Curves around the same time I did. We supported one another, shared the best and worst of times, laughed a lot, and became best of friends helping one another with our businesses.

There were times during the first few weeks when I honestly did not know if I was driving home or driving to the club. In just 2 weeks we had signed up over 100 ladies/members!!! Thankfully, my mother agreed to come to Dallas for a month to help me with the kids while I opened and trained my new staff. There was no way I could have done it without her. The business flourished for 10 plus years. I was extremely blessed to have wonderful women working for me.

I loved getting to know the different ladies who came into the club. I loved the camaraderie and support we gave one. We laughed, we cried. We experienced births, deaths, divorces and marriages together. I truly loved when they reached their goals and we celebrated them loudly!

One of the lessons learned from starting a business, is the necessity to give up some control. I was the oldest child and I had a husband who traveled Monday through Friday, sometimes Sunday through Friday. I was used to being in control out of necessity. The first time I had to let my employee close the club for me, I was a wreck! I worried, "Would she remember to shut everything off? Would she remember to put the alarm on?" My stomach was in knots. One way or another, my body needed a break and guess what? The sun still came up and it set each day! Ha! Ha! Lesson learned.

I was also doing my own QuickBooks, including payroll. Why? It was not my strength. I should have been concentrating on growing the business. Once I handed over those reigns to the professionals, there was no looking back! After all, I was receiving the reports each month. That is all I really needed.

I have always been willing to listen to the opinions of my staff, after all... they are working the floor day after day. I also think it is important to get honest feedback from your customers. At Curves, I did this by placing a comment box in the restrooms. If you are open and you listen to your staff, you listen to your customers... you will be more apt to be successful because you will have a pulse on what is needed.

What has being in business for myself done for you?

It truly allowed me to be home with my children. It allowed me the flexibility to work around their schedules. It also showed me that I have a lot of different talents and that nothing is impossible with hard work and study.

What was the biggest obstacle you've encountered since being in business? How did you overcome it?

In all businesses, there are going to be unexpected setbacks. Shortly after opening, I received a call on a Monday morning from my employee. Apparently the toilet had leaked over the weekend and the club was flooded from the back of the club all the way up to the front door. I asked my employee to put a note on the front door telling our members and potential members what had happened, explaining that we were working hard to remedy the situation that we appreciated their patience. I asked her to also include our telephone number so that the members and/or potential members could call the club for daily updates.

I quickly changed the outgoing voicemail message, fed my children breakfast, drove them to pre-school, and headed to the club. When I pulled in front of the club, I could not believe my eyes. The front windows were completely fogged from the moisture. I opened the door and immediately sunk into the wet carpet. My employee started to cry. I hugged her and told her luckily nobody had been hurt and that this would pass.

I visited all the business within the shopping center asking each business owner or manager if they had ever experienced a flood. One of the owners had and she recommended a company who could come in with dryers. I paid extra to get double the normal blowers and miraculously we were up and running 3 days later. We even signed members up during the drying period at a table and chairs we dragged out the front door!

From the beginning, I trained my employees to treat all members with respect and honor. We were to be empathetic to each and every woman who walked in the door, realizing that we did not know what each woman's "story" was. My psychology classes and behavior modification training were coming in handy. Every woman was to be greeted and every woman was to be thanked sincerely, for coming in. The club was to be extremely clean and all equipment maintained to the highest of standards. The approach worked and we grew so fast that we started to bust at the seams.

I quickly needed more space, but my members did not want me moving too far. Luckily there was a woman who owned a gymnastic center in the front of the center who also was busting at the seams. She wanted to move to a larger space, but had to fulfill her existing lease. She and I met and we got along immediately. We were both busy businesswomen and mothers. On a handshake we made plans to have me sublet her space until her lease was fulfilled, pending the landlord's approval.

I asked my staff and my members what they would like to see at the new location. Based on the comments and the direction the company was going, we added a meeting room for seminars, weight loss classes, etc. I also added a suggestion box but placed it in the restrooms so comments could truly be anonymous! After moving into our new space, I received another frantic call that the ceiling in the bathroom had collapsed due to a leak on the roof and the entire club was flooded. This time... I simply hit the repeat button and knew that all would be fine!

Now you probably think that the floods in my Curves were probably the biggest obstacles I have faced in business... not so. You see, while all this was going on, our oldest son started attending Colorado State University as a business major and was working part-time at a cute breakfast and lunch restaurant called The Egg & I Restaurant. He loved it and loved the owners so much that he changed his major, graduated and started working for a well-known restaurant chain in Dallas.

The Egg & I Restaurant had decided to franchise and they offered our son the opportunity to return to Colorado to manage one of their stores. After two years, our son approached me and my husband, to see if we wanted to purchase a franchise location in Dallas for The Egg & I Restaurant. I did not want a restaurant. It is the absolute hardest business to run, let alone be successful. I was running my Curves, raising two small children, and I reminded our son that his father was traveling Monday through Friday. I just could not add anything more to my plate. Our son worked hard at convincing us that it would work. He would completely run the restaurant and we did not have to do a thing but finance the business. He and my husband teamed up and started selling it as a wonderful way for us to build up a nest egg for retirement. We then went to visit the Management Team of Egg & I Holdings in Colorado. We met at one of The Egg & I Restaurants and after tasting their food, and listening to what a great manager our son was, looking into the new management team's background, I agreed with my husband and son to open a restaurant in Texas.

Our first The Egg & I Restaurant opened in Addison/North Dallas, Texas in July 2008. It was an exciting time. Our daughter-in-law became pregnant and our first grandchild was born in September 2008. We were so proud of our son who was doing an amazing job of running the restaurant.

However, setbacks like I mentioned before, will occur. In October, 2008 the stock market crashed and consumers stopped spending money on anything they perceived as "extra" such as going out to eat or gym memberships. Curves was holding its own because of our "niche" and our incredible staff. However, the restaurant started feeling the effects immediately. We were the first The Egg & I Restaurant in Dallas, so we had absolutely no brand presence. In mid-December, 2008 we were devastated by the loss of my brother. He was an incredible human-being and a friend to all that knew him. We were very close and it was hard to believe that he was gone.

Two weeks later I received a call from our bank letting me know that our credit card processing system had been hacked into at our restaurant. The bank told me that they would be confiscating all monies received via credit card purchases until the responsible party was determined. In the meantime, we would have to get a cashier's check for $10,000.00 and immediately have to hire a forensic investigator to determine if we were responsible in any way. I was still in shock over the loss of my brother and did not truly comprehend what they were telling me. I told them that I had gotten every other word and that they needed to repeat everything. I soon realized that until we were proven innocent, every time a customer came in to eat and paid with a credit card, the money would be sent right to the bank. We would not get paid. I asked them how we were supposed to survive without making any money, and they simply said to do our best - not exactly the answer I was looking for. My husband, son and I rallied quickly. I called a family meeting with my son, daughter-in-law and husband at the restaurant. I told them that we were not going down without a fight. I reminded them that we all had decided to go into this business together and that as long as we had each other we would get through this crisis. We had recently experienced the loss of our pastor, my brother and our son lost his grandfather; we were not going to lose our business or home. Everyone agreed.

We strategized and the only way we could survive is if our son did not take a full salary. We would all have to really cut back on expenses and get creative. My husband asked me to please put my attentions toward the restaurant vs. Curves, as it was a much greater investment at stake. I agreed.

I called a meeting with my "angels," as I referred to my staff at Curves, and told them that I had to jump in and help my family with the restaurant business. I would be available by telephone and email but that I was truly going to rely on their incredible talents and loyalty at the club. They were amazing and told me that it was their job and that they completely understood. It was very stressful not being able to be at the club.

We constantly brainstormed for ways to bring in new customers. I started going door-to-door and introducing our restaurant to area businesses. After several days of doing so, it became apparent that catering was needed in our area. I told my son, and he said that The Egg & I Restaurants did not cater. I strongly suggested that we needed to do whatever it took to stay in business and he finally agreed.

We started catering immediately and it truly sustained our business. I also went to an incredible local theatre and asked if they would be interested in In-kind food donations in exchange for advertising. They were very interested and we forged a terrific relationship with them and continued throughout the years. In fact, I recently joined the Board of Directors for WaterTower Theatre in Addison, Texas.

My son and I touched tables at the restaurant to listen to our customers. It was suggested that I attend networking meetings to expand our exposure. So I did. I remember my first networking meeting. It started off pretty easy. I simply introduced myself and talked to different people in the room, telling them about our restaurant.

Then, the facilitator announced that we would begin the meeting with elevator speeches. I had no idea what he was talking about and literally looked around for an elevator! I then looked over at the President of the Boys & Girls Club of North Texas and she could see the look of bewilderment in my eyes. She whispered, "You've got this. Just be yourself and tell everyone about your restaurant like you did with me earlier."

Incidentally, we had always said that if we opened a restaurant near her that we would do an event to benefit her club. We did that this February, and I just gave a speech at her 10 year Anniversary citing her encouraging words at that networking meeting. Building relationships is very, very important.

Networking at various meetings led to starting our own networking group - North Dallas Networking Group (NDNG) in our Meeting Room at our Addison/North Dallas location. I quickly listed our group on Meetup.com and soon we were bringing in business people from all over the area. Almost 6 years later, this group is running strong with integrity-minded members looking for business-to-business and strong referrals, terrific guest speakers, and great business-building sessions. www.meetup.com/north-dallas-networking-group.com.

The lesson here is to listen to your customers and look for a need within your industry. Think outside the box... or I should say, the fishbowl! More importantly, a great product and great service and the feeling that your customer gets when at your establishment outweigh everything else.

It was a very stressful time for all of us to say the least. We truly did not know if we were going to lose the business, let alone our home. We at one point talked about our son, daughter-in-law and grandson moving in with us to reduce costs. Our 12 year-old daughter worked weekends and helped stuff envelopes and staple business cards to menus at home. I started reading industry magazines every chance I could. Our son ran a tight ship and kept the employees motivated and the customers happy which I learned is a hard thing to do in a slow restaurant.

We seemed to be plugging along when on our first Mother's Day, the Super Bowl of days in the restaurant business, a day that could provide the largest sales day to-date, our drains clogged in the kitchen. Water was starting to rise everywhere in the kitchen. We knew we had an opportunity to make a lot of money in one day, so my husband immediately jumped in and squeegeed and dumped water for 5 hours straight. It was like a scene out of Fantasia! Our 12 year-old bussed tables, our son ran the operations of the business, I touched tables, ran food, visited with customers and filled-in where needed. We were exhausted at the end of the day we made it through another crisis and had our largest sales day since opening. The customers never knew what was happening in the kitchen as we maintained EGGcellent food and service.

In August of 2009 the bank and the investigators concluded that the breach was in no way our fault and we were able to get most of our money released minus some minimal penalties from the credit card companies. We had survived one of the worst times of our lives. It is hard to believe that we opened our second restaurant a year later! In July, 2010 we opened our second The Egg & I Restaurant in Carrolton/W. Plano. In October, 2010 welcomed our second grandson! We had all become stronger, closer, and learned that together we could get through any crisis thrown our way.

In 2011, we had another setback. In a series of corporate layoffs, my husband lost his job of 23 years. He asked me if I would please continue to concentrate my efforts to help grow the restaurants. Again, I had a meeting with my Angels at Curves and told them it was with a heavy heart that I needed to sell the club in order to devote time to our family restaurant business. My Curves franchise agreement was up and it did not make sense to renew. They all understood and only asked that I make sure that whoever bought the club be a good person to work for. I put a letter up in the club at the close of business on Saturday and first thing Monday morning I received the first of many calls from one of my members stating that her prayers had been answered. She had just lost her on-line business on Friday and she saw my note and knew it was meant to be. We met that afternoon and I absolutely fell in love with her. She had been working out early mornings so we had never met. We were finishing each other's sentences by the end of our meeting!

There were several other members and outside people who wanted to purchase the business and even offered me more money. However, the members and the staff had become my family and it was not about the money. The new owner was exactly the answer to my prayers. I was so grateful to have such a wonderful person taking over "my" club. We laugh today as we look back on our "handshake" deal and have truly become very fond of one another. We joke that we are sisters from another mister and have a standing "girlfriend date" in January to have lunch. Remember... this was the second "handshake-type" deal I had made. Both were with women of high integrity and strong Christian faith and in both instances, I went with my gut feeling that this was "right".

What was your most rewarding experience since starting your own business?

I look back mostly at the triumphs. All the hard work at Curves paid off when we were able to pay off the startup debt within six months. We were able to put two of our children through college with the money made, and I was lucky enough to experience the joy of thousands of women attaining their personal goals. I met wonderful people and I made lasting friendships. I look back at a period when I thought I might have to simply close the club and I would like to think because I tried to do the right thing -- that all worked out the way it did.

In terms of The Egg & I Restaurant, I would say that being able to open restaurant number two, after almost losing everything was an incredible feeling. We not only made it out of one of the worst periods of our lives, but we were expanding our family business. We then opened restaurant number three and this year, just six years after that very difficult year in our lives, we were presented with The Egg & I Restaurant Franchisee of the Year award! Our son and daughter-in-law have bought into the business and have just bought their 3rd home which allows us to be 10 minutes door –to-door with our grandsons!

We have entered into several other business ventures. Most have been successful and some have not. What I have learned is that life is a series of triumphs and setbacks. It is how we respond to the setbacks that set us apart. I have luckily remained steadfast. It is also very important in business who you surround yourself with. After a very stressful time period this past year regarding a separate business venture, I attended and then served on a Tres Dias weekend, which truly helped to heal me and remind me to lift all my troubles up to God so that it becomes his battle and not just mine. I don't want to give it away for anyone who may attend, but the prayer stone given to me at my last weekend read: STEADFAST.

What 3 things do you now wish you would've known when you started?

People often ask what I would have done differently with my businesses if I could. With regards to Curves I really wished I would have listened to my gut and moved to the town my club was located. It would have been so much easier on me, my family, and my staff had we done so. With regard to the restaurant – the stock market crash and the Internet fraud was out of our control. I certainly knew what I looked for in a restaurant, as a consumer, but the operations of a restaurant itself was very new to me.

Overall, I cannot emphasize the importance regarding the people you surround yourself with. Surround yourself with people of integrity and people who are going to respect you, your staff, your vendors, and your customers.

How do you keep yourself motivated and encouraged when things don't go right?

The setbacks at Curves had prepared me for the worst in realizing that with faith and determination, you can pretty much handle any challenge that comes your way. I have learned that it is critical in regard to who you surround yourself with. Positive, God-loving people will stand by you, lift you up, and work towards a common goal. This pertains not only in my personal life, but also in my professional life.

People hear the story of our early restaurant years and ask how we persevered. I always tell them that faith, family, and my girlfriends have always helped keep me motivated. I would highly suggest you study that all women in business read and study all the industry information you can, listen to your customers, listen to your employees and then go with your gut. When I look back, 9 times out of 10 my gut was spot on.

What's your biggest business goal over the next 12 months and what will you do to meet it?

My short-term goals right now are concentrated on our newest location in Denton, Texas. We have had staffing changes, major operations training, and now are putting a full-court press on PR and networking in terms of bringing awareness and traffic to the restaurant. Our son has been promoted to Area Director which will allow him to focus on growing the Denton business.

A fun aspect of owning the restaurants has been my television and radio spots. I have had the opportunity to appear on several morning television news shows in their cooking segments. I have even appeared on a morning show for Curves. I absolutely love being on television. Absolutely, the word makes me laugh. The first time I was on television for Curves I wanted to be certain that I did not say umm. So instead, I said absolutely. When my friend and I watched the taped show afterwards, I succeeded in never saying Um. However, I had said "absolutely" 27 times!!! We fell off the couch laughing!!! I have had several producers tell me that I have a natural gift and that they wish they had something for me to do at their station. I have had several people comment that I should truly do something in terms of television. I have no interest in becoming famous. It truly is not about that. It is about the camera, the audience, and the entire process. It is very exciting and I am lucky that it comes very natural to me.

After years of my husband telling me that I need to accept that I have a God-gifted talent, I am going for it in my own small way as I believe that there are many stories about women and their struggles and triumphs that we all can learn from. Although I have secured the domain names of the following websites, they are not up and running yet.

However, my goals now include starting a blog, a book, and an Internet talk show about **Steadfast Sheroes. (SteadFastSheroes.org**). It is about women who have remained Steadfast. They have made it through the storms of life with faith and perseverance. These women have truly become Sheroes to those women around them and for other women who can benefit by learning from their experiences and lessons learned.

I would also like to pursue my business passion, *Outside the Fishbowl Looking In* **Consulting. (OutsideTheFishbowl.org**) If you are getting stuck in your business, at home, or both, I can come in and take a fresh look at what seems to be working and not working and work with you to put a plan in place with in terms of systems, employee training, etc. After all, things are much clearer when you are Outside The Fishbowl Looking In! I also want to start a non-profit called **High 5 Productions (High5Productions.org**) in which we can all lend a helping hand, a high five for encouragement, etc. to people in need. Lastly, I have been working on a business called **Nicetees (Nicetees.org**) an inspirational business model that will offer various uplifting and inspirational designs. $1 of each order will be donated to a charitable organization.

I truly believe that giving back and volunteering is very important. Volunteering allows us to see how truly blessed we are. I look forward to volunteering more of my time at organizations such as My Possibilities in Plano, Texas a non-profit that provides day services to adults with disabilities. My husband, daughter and I also love volunteering in the children's ministry at our church, Hope Fellowship. The kids truly brighten my day with their hugs and smiles!

What advice would you give to a woman entrepreneur who is ready to take her business to the next level?

I recommend to all women entrepreneurs that they go visit with a woman in business, whether it be in the same type of business or not and interview her. Make sure you have the same morals, ethics, and business goals as she does before you start taking advice. Ask her what her biggest challenges have been, what she would have done differently, and what advice she can give you. Then research!!!!! Also, have a monetary reserve ready for those things that you do not expect. Remember our very unexpected $10,000.00 forensic investigator fee. A financial setback can cripple you.

One of the biggest struggles women entrepreneurs have is how to price themselves. What advice would you share about pricing your services and offerings?

As women in business, we must remember that if there is no perceived value being given to a product or service, then people are not going to pay. Women are nice in this regard, perhaps too nice— myself included. Approach every situation for yourself as you would for a friend or a loved one, and you will be fair to yourself.

I will tell you that when it came to the build out of some of my businesses, the sub-contractors were not used to working with a woman. I could have taken some of their comments personally, but chose to show them that I was willing to work with them due to their years of experience but would appreciate in return their respecting my opinion. Again, respecting someone will almost always outweigh differences.

What must have resources would you recommend to use in your business?

I would recommend that women entrepreneurs have a good support group both in regards to your industry and among your friends and family. Read everything you can get your hands on about your industry and about growth – related to both business and you personally.

In addition, balance in your life will help you succeed; and downtime is essential both mentally and physically. Be sure to produce a great product, and give the customers great service and a great experience.

What makes you a Woman that Impacts? How are you impacting your world?

I would like to think that I have been a good example for women entrepreneurs and for my children. I believe that through hard-work, perseverance, study, and respect for all that I come into contact with, as well as an attitude of gratitude - you can grow relationships in order to grow your business. Treating those you come into contact with respect and trying to do your best, truly can impact those closest to you and I believe the world. Treat your staff as if they are a part of our family, after all, your business cannot be successful without them.

I always say, "It is simple, treat people the way you would want your children, parents, or your pets to be treated." Always be open to learning new things, listen to your gut, and always give it your best. Be steadfast ladies. Good luck and I hope you become a Steadfast Sheroe!

Continue the Conversation with
Rose McGrane-Colarossi:

Below are the various ways that you can connect with Rose and learn more about what she has to offer.

Websites:
www.TheEggandIrestaurants.com

- Steadfast Sheroes. (SteadFastSheroes.org)
- Outside the Fishbowl Looking In Consulting
- (OutsideTheFishbowl.org)
- High 5 Productions (High5Productions.org)
- Nicetees (Nicetees.org)

Twitter:
www.twitter.com/EggandINDallas

Facebook:
www.facebook.com/pages/The-Egg-I-Addison-Carrollton-Denton/100145770069490

SHERYL JONES
Founder, Rodcor

Tell us a little about yourself. We want to learn about the person behind the brand. Share with us what your business is and why you wanted to start this business.

Hello, I am Sheryl Jones is CEO & Founder of Rodcor Services located in Irving, TX. I am the Queen of Hearts, giving my community TREMENDOUS LOVE. I SERVE adults & children with special needs by providing their families with EXTRAORDINARY STAFF so they can take a much needed break to reduce their STRESS.

My story starts at a difficult time in my life; I was blessed to be a parent of a special needs little boy who taught me so much before his death. It is so important that we learn from our past; our past is there to teach us something. Sometimes we think of our bad situation as a disadvantage; many times that situation turns into a TREMENDOUS advantage in your life. Not many people can honestly say that they have my unique perspective of my field because I have been a parent of a special needs child, a high level manager in the specialized field and now I am a business owner in the same field.

During the times I was providing care for my son, I noticed that there were times in my journey that came up all of the time where I needed someone to discuss things with. Although my mother was a Head Nurse at the VA hospital, she had very little experience with special needs.

I noticed that my situation was very unique, so I sought help. Major tip right here - when you know something is lacking in your life, seek help. I decided that I would bond together with others in my same state, and we helped each other. I remember vividly helping start the support group for children with disabilities and being very active as I learned how to care for this precious child.

I worked at so many companies in Dallas; I was looking for a great company that did it right. I started my business because I saw that most of the companies in the Dallas area operated with NO Heart. I saw so many unmet needs of the families with special needs children that just needed time and attention. Most of the companies had leadership that had no idea the difficulties that the parents of special needs children encounter.

The companies were excellent at getting money and running great businesses; however, product delivery was a little shaky. I brought a unique skill to the table, so I became a "Hot Commodity" in Dallas seeking a team member good at attracting clients because I had a pull like no others. I was sought at by 2 different companies while working elsewhere. I thought this was common; I had no idea I was so SPECIAL. Business tip right here - look different and be confident in your differences.

People will love you or maybe not, and that is what you want. It's important to get attention; with the attention you might get haters, and you will get admiration and people watching you. Focus on the people that make connections with you; from that connection great referrals and genuine business relationships can develop.

When did you know you were meant to launch your own business?

In December 2004, I was placed on a Super User Team at my current job. I was super excited to be trained to run and view all of the reports for my department. Little did I know this would wake up the entrepreneur inside me.

On January 18, 2005, I decided to see how good our 2004 year was in revenue. To my surprise the number was $2,142,301.89. I will never forget this number; you see, I was totally responsible for the entire marketing of this program.

It was a new program that just started in the State of Texas, and I had decided I was going to be an expert for this new program. I wanted everyone in Dallas to come to me to learn about it.

I was shocked when I saw how much I had produced by "running my mouth" with the families in need. On that day I wondered, "Could I do this for myself?" It took 8 more months, but on Sept 3, 2005, I left that stable job. I realized they were paying me so little to produce so much! I was # 2 in revenue for my small department out of this multi-million dollar agency.

What has being in business for yourself done for you?

Being in business has given me courage to live my dreams. My unique experiences, education, difficulties and how I respond to them make me a commodity today. When you decide that all that you have experienced is worth sharing is when you begin to see the making of a company.

All of those times I asked my former company—why can't we provide this to our clients? The answer would be it was not in the budget. Now I provide those perks to my clients. I began to realize that people are drawn to those who give their best. People need others, and they will continue to spread your message if you provide value. Dream huge dreams; I am always looking to increase on what I am giving. I don't believe we can over give; it is important that we understand all aspects of our business, and we do want to make money, but there is nothing like the paychecks from the heart.

If someone asked you, who are your ideal clients, what would you say?

My ideal client would be a mother of an elementary school child with autism, Down syndrome or any disability that she is struggling to get the help with. She would like to go to dinner, but locating a babysitter does not come easy for her. Another ideal client would be that mother who has a child with a disability leaving high school, and she is clueless what his /her transition plan looks like—what's next for that child? I have a unique gift of making complex things simple and helping parents understand the benefit of one plan or another.

How do you measure success and what is your definition of success?

I measure success by the amount of engagement the families have with me. It is a goal of mine to have all of the families know my name and who I am. This reminds me when my mother died; I had several hundreds of messages/cards and several of my clients attended the funeral service - that was shocking to me, but on that day I realized I was making a difference.

I want to ensure that the families know they can contact me when they need something. I want them to see me as a trusted resource for their family. When people see you as a friend it is harder for them to quit on you. They feel like they are leaving a part of their family. The last 3.5 years have been very difficult due to a loss of almost 200 clients. I am called and/or emailed regularly by former clients to see how they can return. I know these families see the value of my service, and they are unpaid commercials for me because of the time and the extras that I provided to them.

What was the biggest obstacle you've encountered since being in business? How did you overcome it?

The biggest obstacle has been attracting enough clients to maintain a healthy business. When you have a specialized field the market of available clients is much smaller than the average population; in Dallas and surrounding suburbs, there are about 3 million people, but in my field only about 25,000 fit the criteria, and my current contract only serves 1,200 of them.

With 1,200 clients being available in the Dallas area there are 68 providers. I know one of the major keys is to look different and run faster. In business you must have a weekly and daily plan of what to do next in order to dominate the market place. It is critical now to STAND OUT in the marketplace because it seems like everyone is going into business.

It's funny, but I have had several people I would have considered friends, learn about my business and became a direct competitor, from the information I have given them. My take on that is WHAT GOD HAS FOR YOU NO ONE CAN TOUCH IT, so I laugh and move on because only the strong will survive.

What have you learned about yourself in running your business?

I have learned that I am a SURVIVOR. It has not been easy, but I stay the course. I will not give up on my dream, and I will not allow others to talk me out of my OUTRAGEOUS Plans. I know I think light years ahead because I know the future is bright and abundance is destined to come my way. My efforts will not be in vain, because I believe I am planting seeds that will reap a HUGE harvest soon. You must always believe, if you don't please do yourself a favor and don't start a business. When you want to throw in the towel, it is that belief that will continue to keep you.

What was your most rewarding experience since starting your own business?

The most rewarding experience has been Celebrating the Invisible. I have a commitment to show the individuals with special needs a unique view of their life. I have shocked so many people with taking the time to honor my clients - just the simple things like birthdays, and holidays seem to set me apart. This is where you can be creative - not many people send mail anymore. I know it is CRITICAL to stand out.

My clients look for my monthly newsletter and call me to see if something is wrong if they don't get it. I believe everyone has a right to be celebrated regardless of their situation. I know that I provide events like no other company in my field. I take pride in providing quality events for quality people.

What 3 things do you now wish you would've known when you started?

The 3 things I wished I would have known were: 1) I wished I would have known that every business has ebbs and flows. I did not know things can change in an instant and if you are not prepared for it, change it can hurt. 2) I wish I would have saved more money and spent less during my early years. I thought money would be flowing forever at the rate my business started. I was not equipped for the huge decline due to a change in presidential party. 3) I wished would have known that success brings "fake friends". I would have guarded my heart more and not gotten so attached to people.

How do you keep yourself motivated and encouraged when things don't go right?

I keep myself motivated and encouraged by going to events and being involved in the Thrive mastermind group. I think everyone needs a coach in life. This journey is not meant to run alone. There are so many areas to learn and explore a new way of looking at issues and concerns. A good coach can help you create, see and seize opportunities. I work on my mindset every Monday-Friday, it can be audio training, books, affirmations or pictures. I know when I am better, my company is better and I want to give my clients the best.

What's your biggest business goal over the next 12 months and what will you do to meet it?

My biggest goal in the next 12 months will be twofold. 1) To become known in the Dallas/Ft. Worth area as an industry leader, and 2) I will build my brand-Queen of Hearts as a speaker. I want my story to be heard by thousands and provide hope to those families in need. I will take charge of my speaking platform, I will train like no other person, I will speak to anyone that requests me, I will ask to speak at various locations, I will dominate my platform and I create my name as Queen of Hearts. The next 12 months, I will become the business woman I have always dreamt of being.

What advice would you give to a woman entrepreneur who is ready to take her business to the next level?

My advice to an entrepreneur woman is to GO FOR IT-DON'T BE SCARED. You must believe that God did not place a dream in your heart without the ability to reach it. If you lack believe in yourself, no one will believe you can accomplish great things. Your main goal is to find customers who are thirsty for what you have to offer, guess what, when a person is thirsty all they want is water and you are the water they need.

Please believe you can quench their thirst. You are the water they are waiting for; they might be drinking somewhere else until you decide I'm providing water now. We your sister entrepreneurs, BELIEVE IN YOU.

One of the biggest struggles women entrepreneurs have is how to price themselves. What advice would you share about pricing your services and offerings?

Since my business is free to my clients, I believe pricing is something that must be discussed with a coach who has demonstrated success with paying clients. Never undervalue yourself. Even if you feel uncomfortable with the price know that the coach has proven experience to know that your market can bear your price.

One of the best things you could do is commit yourself to CANI-Constant and Never-ending Improvement. Your mind is a huge computer, it has the ability to retain and recall a lot of information. Study and prepare yourself for success. You will be happy you spent the time reading books, attending seminars and spending time with other business people. Decide how often you will educate yourself. I am committed to daily education, if you can't do daily, schedule a weekly time to learn, if you can't do weekly at least monthly. If you want a really good business commit to do more.

Most CEO read 4-5 books a month. That's if you want to be AVERAGE, I know that is not YOU. Great CEO's reads or listens to 1-2 books per week. Step up to greatness— anyone can take the time to read.

What makes you a Woman That Impacts? How are you impacting your world?

I am A Woman That Impacts because I am unique because I give love as the Queen of Hearts and I leave a mark on the world as I Celebrate the Invisible. As I help those with special needs shine, I will also help others wanting to walk this Entrepreneurial Journey. Be blessed and be a blessing.

Continue the Conversation with Sheryl Jones:

I am Sheryl Jones, the Queen of Hearts, CEO & Founder of Rodcor Services located in Irving, TX.   I SERVE adults & children with special needs.   What makes my company different is that I have been a stressed out parent of a child with special needs, I've worked closely with families as a social worker and now I own a heart-centered company that provides the services of my dreams by "Celebrating the Invisible".

Below are the various ways that you can connect with Sheryl and learn more about what she has to offer.

Website:
www.rodcor.com

Twitter:
www.twitter.com/ rodcor1sheryl

Facebook:
www.facebook.com/rodcoreducates

SUSAN TOLLES
Founder, The Flourishing Life

Tell us a little about yourself. We want to learn about the woman behind the brand.

My top priorities in life are my faith and my family. First, I am a Christ Follower, growing daily in my walk with Him as I surrender my own plans to the journey He has designed for me. The bolder I am about my authentic self through my faith, the richer my life becomes! My faith is my primary source of confidence, peace and joy and I start every day thanking God for my abundant blessings.

My family also brings such happiness into my life, leaving me in awe of my good fortune. I have been happily married to Jim for 35 years and our dream has come true, as all three of our adult children and their families live nearby in Austin now. We have one precious granddaughter, and two more grandchildren due in February 2015! Our growing family is very tight-knit, and our get-togethers are frequent and fun. Being a grandmother has totally changed my perspective on what is really important, and my new priorities have changed my work/personal schedule for the better.

I was adopted at birth, and raised as an only child in East Texas. I searched for my birth mother for 22 years and found my family in 2013. Although the end of that journey was not what I had hoped, I learned so much about myself through the process. I know now that I am enough just as I am, without that "missing piece" I believed I needed for so long. Also, I am so grateful for my life as it has unfolded and have such gratitude for everything I have.

For fun, I love to travel (especially to Italy!), shop, sit on the dock at our getaway home on Lake LBJ and share a glass of wine with friends. One little-known tidbit is that I am a scuba diver, and love to explore the magnificent undersea world.

Share with us what your business is and why you wanted to start this business. When did you know you were meant to launch your own business?

When my oldest daughter was born, Jim and I decided that I would leave my job in the financial world to stay home and raise our children. Little did I know, I would be in that role for 24 years! Throughout that time, I tried to be super-mom, super-wife, super-volunteer and super-caregiver, as I devoted my life to serving others. I took on many part-time roles within the community, from children's ministry coordinator to school board president. As I look back, I see how each of those positions has prepared me for my midlife reinvention and has been–part of the divine progression toward where I am today.

When I was 52, I reached a major crossroads that changed my life. My children were all away at college, I had resigned from the school board, and my mother had just passed away. I was no longer needed as a mom, leader or caregiver and my loss of identity hit me hard. Who was I, and what would I do the rest of my life? I knew I had many productive years ahead, but was paralyzed by fear and overwhelmed by the thought of going back to the workplace.

I searched for resources for women over 50 and found very few, so I decided to create my own! On February 1, 2010 I launched FlourishOver50.com with no experience in publishing or web design and it has been an amazing journey since then. I have connected with women all over the world who want the same things in life—purpose, passion and beautiful legacies from our midlife reinventions.

I spent the rest of 2010 working constantly to build my web traffic, with the goal of being on the first page of Google®. I concentrated on generating content, keywords, social media and article marketing to expand my brand, and put in hundreds of hours toward my vision that included advertisers and sponsors for my top-ranked online magazine for women. I was so consumed by comparing myself to my competitors that I lost sight of my true goals. By December of that year, I had made it to the first page of

Google® but I was drained, and had lost sight of *why* I was doing what I was doing.

I took a much-needed break, did some deep soul searching, and realized that I had jumped into the venture because it was a good idea, not because I had a clear mission or plan for success. I had also been doubting my *own* abilities, as I had believed that I needed to stay in the background of the website and promote other authors instead of letting my own brilliance shine. In my conversations with God, He revealed that I needed to get out from behind my computer to fully use the gifts He had given me; the ones I had used sporadically over the years as I lived out my life's calling "to inspire joy by awakening worth."

Since that time, I have become a Certified Life Purpose Coach®, a professional speaker and author, and now use my website as a means to reach my goals, not the primary goal. I have expanded beyond Flourish Over 50® and now guide women entrepreneurs to live, lead and succeed with purpose through VIP coaching and programs that I have written. The Flourishing Life® is my new platform, and it allows my authentic self to shine as I blend life, faith and career in my role as a coach. I am also the Austin Market Director for the Mentoring Women's Network®, connecting professional women in Central Texas with a nationwide network of women supporting one another through mentoring relationships, training and mastermind groups. If I had not fully embraced my immense value as a coach, mentor and leader, I would still be hiding behind my computer every day, not reaching my full potential.

What has being in business for yourself done for you?

One of my favorite quotes is from Howard Thurman, an influential African American author, philosopher, theologian, educator and civil rights leader, who said "Don't ask what the world needs. Ask what makes you come alive, and go do it. Because what the world needs is people who have come alive." I truly believe I have come alive as a Life Purpose Coach and professional speaker, as I am creating a rich legacy in this chapter of my life. My confidence has soared and I have a priceless contentment now. It hasn't always been an easy road, but I cannot imagine a better life than what I have today. And to think, it all took off in my 50's!

Another benefit of being in business for myself has been the friendships I have developed over the past few years. I have been inspired, supported and challenged by women who want the best for me, and I have many girlfriends around the globe who I know I can always depend on.

If someone asked you, who are your ideal clients, what would you say?

My ideal client is a woman who wants to live according to her life's purpose and who is intentional about creating and implementing a plan to step fully into who she was created to be. She wants to live a balanced life, putting her faith and family first as she builds a fulfilling career. I especially love guiding a woman entrepreneur in translating her life purpose into the mission and goals for her business, creating a foundation for sustained success. Because I have reinvented myself from mom/caregiver/volunteer to coach/mentor/entrepreneur, I also have so much valuable personal experience and wisdom to share as a mentor. I help all women shed their self-sabotaging beliefs to find greater confidence and less doubt as they acknowledge their value as a precious child of God.

How do you measure success and what is your definition of success?

When I first began, I measured my success by my Google® ranking, but when I got there, I didn't feel as though I had "arrived." Measuring my worth by comparing performance numbers certainly was not fulfilling, and it didn't bring the avalanche of sponsors I'd envisioned. Today, I define success as making a difference in the lives of women, one at a time, with a heart-centered approach. So many of them begin our journey feeling lost, confused and without purpose. They want to have a more meaningful life, but don't know where to begin! Being part of the "aha moment" when they experience clarity and say "That's it!" is so rewarding, and hearing "I couldn't have done this without you" affirms that I am fulfilling my divine calling. When I speak, whether it is for a group of 20 or 2,000, if I make an impact on just one person, then I count it as a successful day. Who knows what the ripple effect will be?

In my role with Mentoring Women's Network®, my success is in connecting women with mentors who will share their knowledge and wisdom in a unique way. Creating mastermind groups for entrepreneurs or women within a corporate structure creates a powerful synergy as they learn from one another and from our mentors. Women in leadership roles will play an integral part of our future economic success, and providing professional development and mentoring for these leaders is exciting for me.

What was the biggest obstacle you've encountered since being in business? How did you overcome it?

My biggest obstacle has actually been myself! In the beginning, I had such low self-confidence and thought I would simply be a connector between women who were looking for resources and experts who had the information.

Eventually I realized that *I am the expert*, and I didn't need to spend all my time promoting others. As I have grown as a life coach and speaker, I have learned to value my personal experiences and wisdom by fully embracing my unique gifts. I still battle self-doubt, and when I think I am finally settled in with a plan, God shakes things up and tells me I am playing too small yet again. This beautiful quote from Marianne Williamson is a constant reminder that I must get out of my own way and shine brilliantly.

"… Who am I to be brilliant, gorgeous, talented, fabulous? Actually, who are you not to be? You are a child of God. Your playing small does not serve the world. There is nothing enlightened about shrinking so that other people won't feel insecure around you. We are all meant to shine, as children do."

What have you learned about yourself in running your business?

When I began this journey, I believed I didn't have much to offer the world. I had been a stay-at-home mom for 24 years, and had failed to acknowledge that all I had done during that time had contributed to my being skilled and valuable. Stepping way out of my comfort zone, taking risks and lots of prayer has increased my confidence exponentially. Discovering my purpose and embracing my God-given gifts have shown me that I am already equipped with everything I need to fulfill my calling. Instead of shrinking behind the curtain of an introvert, I have continued to push myself to new heights, which is sometimes uncomfortable, but always rewarding. Now, instead of saying "why me?" when approached for a new adventure, I say "why not!"

Another part of my personal growth has been letting go of things that are not the best use of my time. In the beginning, I tried to do it all—HTML coding on my website, graphics and managing the editorial calendar for Flourish Over 50. For a while, I even had three websites going! I finally realized that just because I *could* do something didn't mean I needed to do it. Now, instead of spending my precious time on administrative details, I ask for help. I have simplified with one site, and outsource whenever possible. That is not easy for a perfectionist, but it has given me more time to enjoy what I am doing, both professionally and personally!

What was your most rewarding experience since starting your own business?

When I launched FlourishOver50.com, I wanted to celebrate with a party. I didn't know if many people would come, but I knew that at least ten of my friends would! My launch party was held at a beautiful art gallery with vintage furniture and large paintings of women having fun together in various scenes. I hired a caterer, and the food was beautifully displayed and delicious. But the best part was that 45 women came, and I didn't know half of them! They were friends of friends who had heard about something new for women over 50, and they came to help me celebrate. That evening was magical, and on the way home, I cried, realizing that I had done something really big that had to keep going. Some of those women are now my best friends, and I am so grateful that they have been with me since then.

That party was just the beginning of my own reinvention, and my vision has grown much larger since then. From reaching women around the globe with my website to coaching individual clients, the lessons of that evening still ring true: women want to help one another succeed, to encourage and push us higher, and to be our steadfast travel partners on the journey of life.

What 3 things do you now wish you would've known when you started?

1.) Know your purpose, and let it guide everything you do. I took a giant leap of faith when I launched FlourishOver50.com, implementing an idea because it seemed like a great thing to do. But after that first year I was exhausted, overwhelmed and confused. When I took a break to do some soul searching, I read books by Jack

Canfield, Tony Robbins, John Maxwell and Rick Warren for insights into what made them successful. The common thread among them was *purpose,* which should be at the core of your personal and professional goals.

That was a new concept for me, and once I learned what my true purpose was and how it aligned with my God-given gifts and what I loved to do, I was on a new trajectory that took me confidently beyond my original plan. Knowing my purpose has given me clarity, and a great reason to say "no" more often! Now, I am even more focused on purpose as a Certified Life Purpose Coach® with a deep desire to guide others to reach their full potential.

2.) You must be willing to invest in yourself if you want to be successful. The world is full of powerhouse coaches and self-help gurus who have do-it-yourself programs that they promise will make you rich. I have quite a few of those programs on my shelves, having previously thought that I could not afford to hire one to work with me individually. I eventually admitted that I need the ongoing support and accountability of a coach to help me strategically plan each year instead of trying to do everything on my own. The times when I have worked with business coaches have been my most productive as they challenge and motivate me while providing expert guidance that keeps me focused.

3.) It will take longer than you think, but the winding road will make you infinitely better. When I began, I had a totally different vision for my new career and how quickly I would become successful. That plan has been "upgraded" several times as I have continued to grow and value myself. The journey has been challenging and long but fruitful, and I would not trade it for anything. I know that everything I have done has been well worth the time and resources, and I am in a much better place because I didn't rush. The keys are trust, faith, perseverance, and knowing that God designed this journey before I was even born. His plans are better than mine, and the obstacles I have face were meant to provide insights and experiences that equipped me to better serve others.

How do you keep yourself motivated and encouraged when things don't go right?

On an ongoing basis, I pray and journal, reflecting back on what I have written in the past, so I can see how far I have come. It is in acknowledging the many answered prayers that I can reaffirm the path I am on. I have several devotionals I read daily, and they always seem to speak to me just where I am, and provide the encouragement I need.

I also lean on my girlfriends who are also entrepreneurs when I feel like quitting. I will call one for a quick dose of motivation, or have lunch with several of them so we can share stories and lift one another up. Sometimes I read the testimonials that former clients have written and know that I must keep persevering. Knowing that I have changed lives just by following my own calling gives me energy and enthusiasm.

What's your biggest business goal over the next 12 months and what will you do to meet it?

I will focus on blending my coaching and mentoring roles under my brand as The Flourishing Life®, inspiring and empowering women to flourish in their life, faith and career. As a coach and professional speaker, I will bring purposeful living to my clients and audiences through online programs, VIP coaching, workshops and keynote speeches. To grow Mentoring Women's Network® in Austin, I will present monthly complimentary workshops, meet with key decision-makers in companies, network with professional organizations who want to provide enhanced benefits to their members, and ask for help along the way— a key step that is essential in business development.

Personally, the next five months will be filled with total joy as we welcome two grandchildren—a boy and a girl— and a new daughter-in-love. With so much excitement in my life, how can I not claim success?

What advice would you give to a woman entrepreneur who is ready to take her business to the next level?

Surround yourself with a Personal Board of Directors who will be your problem-solvers, accountability partners, cheerleaders and trusted advisors. These are people who have gone before you and can help you avoid wasting time and energy as you create and execute your plan. Hire a coach who can guide you in strategic planning, goal setting and overcoming self-sabotage. Have several mentors in different areas who will share their experience and wisdom. Participate in a mastermind group with like-minded entrepreneurs, soaking in their keen insights and knowledge as you grow your vision and skills. When you are at a crossroads, these advisors will give you wise counsel for making a decision. When you are discouraged, they will lift you up. And when you reach major milestones, they will be there to celebrate your success! Just think of it as a cross-country trip, which is much more fun when accompanied by friends!

One of the biggest struggles women entrepreneurs have is how to price themselves. What advice would you share about pricing your services and offerings?

Women have such trouble charging what they are worth! We want to give everything away and are afraid to acknowledge the true value we bring to others. If you change lives with your services, that is priceless! If you provide ways to simplify, organize, or attain better health, then you are making a lasting impact that will affect not only your clients, but also their families, their businesses and their communities. Consider your far-reaching influence and claim it.

Look around at what others in your field are charging and don't be afraid to set comparable rates. But let the comparisons end there! Just because you don't have as much experience doesn't mean you are less valuable. You are skilled and as passionate about your services as they are, so act like it!

Try "reverse engineering" to arrive at a target price. How many hours per week/month do you want to work? What is your desired monthly income? How many programs/products do you need to sell to support your financial goals? Doing the math will provide a good starting point. Keep that number high enough to give you some room for flexibility, should you want to offer someone a "quick action" discount or to have a promotional sale.

Finally, consider the perceived value based on price. Studies have shown that people will select a higher-priced option because they believe it will deliver superior quality and better results. This is true from generic grocery products to executive coaching. If someone truly wants to transform her life, then she wants the best person to guide her, not the cheapest.

What must have resources would you recommend to use in your business?

Of course, my number one resource is Mentoring Women's Network®! Every woman needs mentors to help her grow personally and professionally, and this is the perfect place to find people who will meet those needs. We have local markets across the nation, but you can take advantage of our programs no matter where you live. With virtual sessions, you can learn from men and women all over the nation who are ready and anxious to support your journey.

Great books to prepare for entrepreneurship are *The E-Myth Revisited: Why Most Small Businesses Don't Work and What to Do About It* by Michael Gerber and *Think and Grow Rich* by Napoleon Hill.

For great resources, inspiration and support, consider joining iBloom (www.iBloom.co) or National Association of Christian Women Entrepreneurs (www.NACWE.org).

My favorite business tools are

- Hootsuite for social media
- Leadpages for sales and landing pages
- oDesk.com and Elance.com for expert freelancers—from graphic design to transcribers and copywriters—who are super-affordable
- Camtasia for recording webinar presentations
- Clickwebinar for presenting those recordings
- Talkshoe for free live teleclasses (no video)
- Legalzoom for creating your LLC or trademarking your name

What makes you a Woman That Impacts? How are you impacting your world?

I am impacting the world from a global perspective, with a website for women over 50 that had over 100,000 visits a month, and I have had the privilege of speaking to audiences with hundreds of men and women, sharing my strategies and inspiration for more purposeful living. But it all comes down to transforming lives one at a time as I live out my own life purpose "to inspire joy by awakening worth." Guiding a woman to connect with her purpose, overcome self-sabotage and confidently pursue her heart's desires has far-reaching ripple effects through her family, her career and her community. It's like the tiny acorn that grows into a magnificent oak—each of plants those seeds and a hundred years from now people are still benefitting from our work.

Closer to home, I am impacting the world through the legacy I will leave behind. I have three amazing children who love God, live with integrity, cherish family and work hard. When I asked them recently, "What was it about growing up in our home that made you the adult you are today?" their answers were consistent: We had a solid foundation of faith, unconditional love, and respect for one another, and my husband and I were very involved in their lives when they were young. I know they will carry out those same values as they raise their children, and that will influence many generations to come.

Continue the Conversation with Susan Tolles:

Susan Tolles is The Reinvention Strategist for Professional Christian Women, whose clients surround the globe. She is a passionate advocate for professional women, equipping and motivating them to envision more and reach higher, building a career they love without sacrificing their personal wellbeing. Susan's expert guidance leads them to acknowledge their unique value, follow their life's purpose, and lead with confidence and authenticity, with a strategic plan for success by their own design.

Below are the various ways that you can connect with Susan and learn more about what she has to offer.

Website:
www.theflourishinglife.today

Twitter:
www.twitter.com/susantolles

Facebook:
www.facebook.com/susan.tolles

YVONNE GEORGE
Fashion Stylist

Tell us a little about yourself. We want to learn about the person behind the brand.

I am a woman on a mission to get my message across that beauty starts from within. The effect of positive thinking is underrated by most of us. I feel as though it is my place to start changing that through my Fashion and voice. I go back to a quote Audrey Hepburn said "That the beauty of a woman is not in the clothes she wears, the figure that she carries, or the way she combs her hair... The beauty of a woman is seen in her eyes, because that is the doorway to her heart, the place where love resides... True beauty in a woman is reflected in her soul." I love fashion and always have, but people are my passion and that is what makes my job so gratifying. Every day I get to wake up and do both and that is very satisfying.

I am an inspired freelance Fashion Stylist in the Dallas Ft. Worth area. Starting at the age of 16, I worked in high end retail stores. I am known for my Shimmer Shine and Sparkle and that is something that defines who I am and what I am all about. Now, understand I know not everyone wants to wear rhinestones and bling, but they can sparkle and shine in who they are by wearing their own style and being confident in who they are.

After I graduated from high school I attended Wade's Fashion Institute at the Dallas Market Center. After getting my degree in Fashion Merchandising & Design I quickly advanced to the World Trade Center representing some of the top designers in LA, New York and Chicago. Going to school and working at the trade center really opened my eyes up to a whole new world filled with endless possibilities.

After taking some time off to have a family and raise my 3 kids it was time to go back to work. So I sat down with one of my friends and trusted mentor Kathy Eppley, to figure out where I was going to go after being out of the industry for a while. I had actually thought that I might just be someone else's personal assistant.

My friend Kathy said.... "ABSOLUTELY NOT!" Ha! Ha! After knowing me for years she knew that my voice and passion was something I needed to live out in a very expressive way. That was when I decided to launch my very own business. We still laugh about that today and I am so thankful that I had friends in my life who really knew me and knew there was so much more in my life that I had not tapped into yet!

That seed was planted in my head and from there my business was born. Little did I know then that so many opportunities and so many wonderful people were about to enter my life and change it forever. When I am not working I spend most of my time off with family and friends listening to music and traveling.

Share with us what your business is and why you wanted to start this business.

Here is the truth. Every woman wants to look good, but not every woman has the time, energy, or the know-how. That is where I come in and educate and empower women and men. As a personal stylist and fashion expert I help as many people as humanly possible create that "look" that not only helps you look good, feel good but it helps you to reach your full potential in life!

My business is very unique in nature because of all the different services that I offer. As a fashion stylist I coordinate outfits for anyone from a stay at home mom to high profile celebrities. I am a fashion show coordinator as well, so I coordinate fashion shows to introduce all the new up and coming styles of the season.

Additionally, I offer personal shopping services as well. I have clients who do not like to shop nor do they have time to shop so I go and do all the buying for them to save them time. Then I work with them privately at their home in making selections.

I own and operate an online store as well that carries a selection of clothing and accessories. Also, I travel and host trade shows all over by setting up my own travel boutiques when I am on the road. Over this past year my business has made another shift as well and I have started speaking on transforming women from not just the outward beauty but the inward beauty as well.

I wanted to start my business because I truly felt called to do what I love. People are busier than ever before and just don't have the time to shop and they want to look good. My job makes it easier for them, plus I get to stay on top of what the latest fashions trends are and give them an insight into what are the fashion trends of the season.

When did you know you were meant to launch your own business?

The timing was right for me. All my kids were all grown up and going off to college except for my daughter who will be going into high school this year. I had done my first important job which was to be their mom first and foremost and raise them.

The opportunity presented itself when people began asking me to help them with their wardrobe and put their outfits together. I have always been that person that people have come to that needed to feel better about themselves or just needed plain and simple fashion advise. These days there are many more women working and they do not have the time to shop like they used to. I realized that shopping and talking with people gave me so much energy and filled my cup.

When I launched my business everything just clicked and seemed like it was just meant to be. EVERYTHING I did kept leading to another opportunity. Even people I had known 25 years ago I reconnected with and started working with them again. It was as if I had never left. I felt so blessed that they even remembered me and wanted to work with me again after all this time. It was now MY time to put my God-given talent to work and let me begin a new chapter in my life where there was no limit of what my capabilities are. This girl was now "ON FIRE!"

What has being in business for yourself done for you?

One of the main things that I have learned is that great things never come from comfort zones. I had to get out of my own box and find the discipline, courage and commitment to achieve my dream. For the first time in a long time I was not seen as just a mom, but now as mom the business woman.

My kids had seen me actually volunteer and work in their school doing things for them, but they never saw me in my profession. It was important to me as well that they saw this other side of me that wanted to influence the world around me and make a difference.

My business has given me the opportunity to actually be the real Yvonne and have the freedom to do what I love. It allows me to be my own boss and make my own schedule so that I still can be there for my kids when they do need me.

I have realized that I am much stronger, braver and more creative than I ever thought I could be. Being in my business has also helped build my own self confidence even more as well. When you are in business for yourself, you have to get out there and meet people and network. I used to have a hard time meeting people I did not know until I started actually having fun talking about what it is I do. In my job as a fashion stylist there are no two days alike and everyday there is something new and exciting going on. I realized that living my life of passion has helped me fulfill my life purpose. I can't think of anything more rewarding when you know you have truly found your calling. There is never a day that my job feels like work because I love it that much!

If someone asked you, who are your ideal clients, what would you say?

My ideal clients are women between the ages of 25-79. Yes, I actually have a client who is 79 and lives in California. Hi Martha McKay! That list contains many moms, executives, entertainers, life coaches, students, and speakers.

My ideal client is looking for the whole package on how they can create that special look that is just for them. They want the mindset that comes along with it as well. They are the people who want to fully live their life of purpose and are on a mission to not only find it, but live it!

They always want something unique and different and not like everyone else. They must be willing to make small changes, whether it is a new updated wardrobe, new look, small changes to their attitude or just how they go about the way they think. The mind is a very powerful thing and something about us as women, is that we listen to the lies we tell ourselves that "we can't wear that" or that we "can't do that". I want to work with those clients who want to find that sparkle and be excited about who they are! I recently started working with men as well and have found that they usually know what they want, but just need a little guidance as to how to pull it all together.

How do you measure success and what is your definition of success?

Success is growth, development and achieving what you have set out to do. It is a feeling of accomplishment in your greatest achievements. For me, it is all about having that inner peace and the will power to set out to do something that you have never done before. I truly believe you can do anything you want if you apply yourself and have the persistence to see if through all the way to the end. And, you have to have the right mindset.

Don't be afraid to fail. Be afraid not to try. I tell this to people all the time. I was not always like this. I had to learn a different way of thinking and when I did everything began to shift. My whole world began to change.

For me, I visualize where I want to go and I do everything I can to achieve it. For me, it is not about how much money you make, but how happy you are doing what you enjoy and how many lives you touch. Success for me is when I have accomplished something new in my business that I did not know how to do before.

How do you make other's feel? Did you make someone smile today? Are you adding value to the lives of others? Have you reached your goals? It is about doing what you love and seeing your dream come to fruition and being able to share that with other people and truly make a difference in the lives of so many others.

What was the biggest obstacle you've encountered since being in business? How did you overcome it?

Technology has been my biggest downfall since starting my business. I was never really good on the computer and only knew a few basic things just to get by when I started my business. Boy, did that have to change! I knew I should have paid more attention in computer class growing up! Ha! Ha!

However, it is a vital role in any business these days and I believe that you should always be on the cutting edge of technology for that is what will set you apart from the rest. I had to learn what I did not know, but what I found out was that the computer was very forgiving and that there is usually more than one way to do something. Not to mention I had to take a few classes to learn about things that I did not know.

I am constantly having to learn new things because technology is ever changing. I do not think I have exactly overcome it, but I have adjusted to it and learned to "ASK FOR HELP!" Do not get overwhelmed, just do what you can to learn. I promise you will look back over the year and think to yourself "look how far I came."

It is necessary that you have the resources to help you deal with situations when they arise. That is why it is so important to build a team around you to help get through these moments. Relax and just breathe for this too shall pass... or at least until the next one! Ha! Ha!

What have you learned about yourself in running your business?

I have learned that running a business for yourself is very empowering and rewarding. I had no idea I had all this bottled up energy that I had not even tapped into yet. I feel like I was a flower that had not yet bloomed and day by day each pedal was opening up farther and growing into something beautiful.

I have learned that my voice matters. I realized how important it was to be able to play a role in someone's life where they not only look good, but they felt good as well. We all have those days where life beats us down and we don't feel our best about how we look, what we are wearing or even sometimes what we are doing. It is my job as a stylist to help build that self-esteem and encourage them to work on the beauty within.

People are watching you in your business even when you don't think they are. That is why it is so important to be a woman of principle and be who you say you are. These days I am no longer afraid to get out of my comfort zone and meet new people. I know now more than ever that all the wonderful opportunities that have come my way came because I took a chance, got out there and just let people see the real me. I knew that God would place the right people in my path and He did time after time. I look back now where I was when I started and I have come so far, but I am more excited about where I am going.

What was your most rewarding experience since starting your own business?

Definitely, I would say getting to connect with women from all over the world and learning so much about them and what they do has been so rewarding. Specifically, for me meeting country entertainer Penny Gilley and being invited on her TV show to talk about my fashions and getting to travel with her has been a huge blessing in my life. They say there are no accidents and I truly believe that God placed her in my life. She has now become one of my best friends and has been with me through my entire journey as a stylist. I get to travel with her and meet so many other entertainers that it has made for quite an exciting life!

I thrive on getting to know people and my life has been greatly impacted by many of them. It is always so rewarding when I know I had a part in someone's life for a special event where they had worn something from my online store or an outfit that I put together for them to make them feel beautiful. I have built up my relationships now with so many of them. They really value my opinion and they are always calling or texting me to ask for advice on either what to wear or they just need to talk to someone who is going to encourage and inspire them when they need it most.

My clients become my friends and I always do my best to make them feel comfortable where they can open up and we can break down those barriers that keep them stuck in their own life. When I see the impact, the change in their mindset, not to mention their whole outlook on how they see themselves change it really gives me a feeling of overwhelming happiness!

What 3 things do you now wish you would've known when you started?

Being organized is not only helpful, but that it is essential. It is so important to have systems in place to keep track of it all. I believe the second thing would be is to believe you can teach yourself things a lot easier than you think you can. It does take time to learn new things, but the payoff is so much greater. I took so much pride in learning how to add products and work my own e-commerce store.

I was overwhelmed in the beginning, but was determined to not let technology scare me. Lastly, to believe more in myself. You see, we are all capable of so much more and our vision for ourselves is very limiting based on the knowledge we think we have. Anything can be taught, it just takes time and effort. I was brave enough to finally step out into the business but had no idea the impact I was going to truly have on so many peoples' lives.

I have no regrets in life just lessons learned and that is how I look at it every day!

How do you keep yourself motivated and encouraged when things don't go right?

I truly believe success in life comes when you simply refuse to give up, and you have strong goals, any obstacles, failure and loss only act as motivation. To keep motivated I surround myself with like-minded friends and life coaches who encourage me and inspire me.

I have so many mentors in my life that I look up to and who have gone before me in the fashion industry so they share what they did wrong. I listen to them and try and learn from their mistakes. I attend as many seminars and workshops that I can that are empowering and share what I learn with countless others who in return build me up.

I constantly try to stay in a very positive environment and I stay away from negativity period. I do work out and run as well because this is a stress reliever for me and doing so clears my brain and it takes my focus off my problems and gives me a mental break as well.

My faith is very important to me and so I spend time in prayer and talk to God and ask Him to give me wisdom and clarity when things are challenging. We all have things that don't go just the way we planned for them too, that is to be expected, but I try and learn from those mistakes and forgive myself and just move on. Pray about it first, pick up the phone and call one of my mentors, lifelong trusted friends or business coach. Then I refuel and take time to recharge by doing something for myself whether it is going to a spa, taking a walk, listening to music or simply just meditating and being silent.

What's your biggest business goal over the next 12 months and what will you do to meet it?

Goals are so important in a business and must be written down with a date broken down into steps that then becomes your plan of action. For 2015 I have already done that and will be focusing more on that inner beauty. I want to take my business to a deeper level and reach more women and men in helping them "Find their Sparkle."

I will be doing this with a series of videos, workshops and special opportunities for clients to spend one on one sessions with me to really ignite that flame from within and get all fired up to really live life and shine in WHO and WHAT they are in life!

There will be additional marketing to target my specific audiences. My website www.YvonneGeorge.com will undergo and transition into a new and updated website as I begin to brand myself more and target specific audiences. For my online store I will be expanding my clothing and accessories so stay tuned. I am looking forward to new travel opportunities as well speaking and meeting people RIGHT where they are in life.

What advice would you give to a woman entrepreneur who is ready to take her business to the next level?

Don't let FEAR stop you from living your dream. Expect that there will be mistakes along the way and surround yourself with a team of people who will help you reach your goals and help you get there. Always, Invest in yourself because you are worth it and never listen to the chatter of others. You will have people tell you that it can't be done and you just have to go with your own gut and do what you feel is right.

If you have the desire to take it up a notch, then "GO ALL IN!" Do not start something and just do it halfway to see what happens. Make sure you always follow through, but realize there may be some sacrifices along the way. Longer hours, more work, more travel and less time with the family, but keeping it all in balance and perspective is the most important. Again, that is why you need to surround yourself with positive people and again always "ASK FOR HELP!" when needed.

One of the biggest struggles women entrepreneurs have is how to price themselves. What advice would you share about pricing your services and offerings?

I believe that when you are trying to decide on what to charge you really should research what the industry you are in charges and ask yourself, "What is your time worth to you?" If you have a limited belief and do not charge what you are really worth you are cheating yourself. This was my mistake. I love what I do so much I felt like I could do it for free.

However, I have to pay bills, and it costs money to run a business. I soon saw I was not charging enough. When I raised my rates, no one even said anything about it. I was still working the same amount of time, but finally I was actually making the money I needed to make.

Our time is so valuable. That is one of the first questions you should ask yourself early on so that you don't miss out, "what is my time worth?" As you continue to grow in your business, your prices may go up depending on demand, but don't start out selling yourself short! Have several different options for your clients to choose from, so clients with various budgets can work with you. Understand that not everyone is your customer, but know that the ones who do want to work with you will appreciate having a few options to choose from.

What must have resources would you recommend to use in your business?

Get educated first by doing the research and understanding your competition and gaining in depth knowledge of the industry that you are going into. That way, you will be better prepared to make smarter decisions regarding your company. Next, start with a business plan so that you have a clear vision of what your business is going to do and what type of clients you want to attract. It is important to have a blueprint for running and expanding your business. Your business plan contains all of your information about what your business does, the manpower that it will take, as well as financial resources that you will need. Even the most basic home business incurs startup costs, including registering your business name, printing business cards, and buying specific things to run your business. If you have a product based business, you will need resources for that as well.

It is also very vital to have key people to help you run your business, whether that is an employee, personal assistant, marketing company, etc. I learned a long time ago to do what "I DO BEST" and let others "DO THE REST". Countless hours can be lost on bookkeeping, accounting and just the small details of a business, etc. Let someone else pick up the slack for you. Do not try and do it all. As your business expands and you grow, you will soon see that you have to delegate things out and when you do it begins to grow even more.

Last, but not least find a business coach or someone who can help you face the challenges with your business and give you fresh ideas, hold you accountable and encourage you when you need it most. We all need our own cheerleaders to help encourage and inspire! We empower one another!

What makes you a Woman That Impacts? How are you impacting your world?

I believe you should be strong & courageous and take risks and have a full awareness of who you are. I believe in not just talking the talk, but walking the walk. My words mean nothing if I do not have action to follow it up and have accountability. I am comfortable in my own skin and make it a mission to lead by example. I am giving of my time and energy to help others and really want to be there for them and help them feel and look their best. Great women teach and inspire other women. They don't withhold their knowledge they share it!

Continue the Conversation with Yvonne George:

Seen of the Penny Gilley Show on RFD-TV. Yvonne George is a Fashion Stylist in Dallas Ft. Worth, known for her Shimmer Shine & Sparkle! Yvonne has dressed celebrities and high profile individuals, as well as stay at home moms. Her unique sense of style is as beautiful as it is versatile, combining sophistication and elegance. Her dynamic personality and positive energy sets her apart from the rest. She believes everyone should "Find Their Sparkle!"

Website:

www.yvonnegeorge.com

Twitter:

www.twitter.com/ YvonnesFashion

Facebook:

www.facebook.com/yvonnegeorgefashionstylist

JANET BERNSTEIN
Founder, CampStein Photography

Tell us a little about yourself. We want to learn about the person behind the brand.

"Are you keeping the baby?" The nurse at the Rowan Medical Center in Salisbury, North Carolina asked me, about fifteen minutes after showing me the positive blood test I had finally mustered up the strength to take. I had barely registered her question, and my first thought was 'how can I have a baby?'

It was the second of January, 1998, and I had only turned eighteen years old just seven days prior. I remember on my birthday, while visiting my family back home in Texas, how I felt so excited about the future. I knew I was about to embark upon a great adventure, but somehow this wasn't what I had envisioned.

I had graduated a year early, already received my high school diploma, and was supposed to be evaluating colleges in the Charlotte area. I wasn't really sure what I wanted to do, but I had a list of talents and gifts for which I was eager to nurture and share with the world. I wanted to write poetry and stories, and finally enter an 'open mic' night and showcase my singer/songwriter abilities.

I had spent so many years in musical theater, and suddenly flashbacks of my role as Rizzo in Grease came to mind, as I finally felt the emotions of being faced with an unplanned, teenage pregnancy, just as she did. At the tender age of eighteen, I was certainly about to embark upon a great journey into adulthood, though the positive blood test catapulted me into the next chapter of my life that day.

After my brief trip down memory lane, I looked back at the nurse and answered, "Of course I am." My voice had actually cracked a little; perhaps my own body was surprised at the jolt of surety in this former teenage girl turned adult. The nurse smiled at me, and seemed to breathe a sigh of relief over my decision. She gave me some literature on pregnancy and a list of doctors, and wished me the best of luck. Those who know me would probably say I adjust well to change. When I first found out I was going to have a baby, I certainly adjusted quickly. Perhaps my tumultuous childhood actually prepared me for the challenges ahead.

My own mother was diagnosed with several different mental illnesses throughout my childhood, including bipolar, dissociative and borderline personality disorder. She was in and out of hospitals all the time, sometimes following an attempted suicide, or just after a painful experience involving the end of a marriage or relationship or loss of a job.

My mother was married and divorced five times, and we lived in at least 15 different homes or apartments by the time I was seventeen. I attended seven different high schools, and finally my dad allowed me to graduate early, as long as I received a diploma and not a GED. My mother and father divorced when I was only four years old, and I went back and forth between their homes throughout most of my teenage years. My dad was the stability I needed to stay on track both academically and emotionally.

That cold January day, upon leaving the medical center with the biggest news of my life, my biggest fear hit me like a tsunami on a sunny day. I was scared to death to tell my dad about the baby. I didn't fear him or his anger, but I feared his disappointment. My whole life I was told by family how proud they were of my achievements and how the constant moving and changing schools did not deter my desire to succeed. No matter what I witnessed at home, I was determined to push on and be successful. Now I had to admit to the person I admired most that I was not going to look at colleges. I had to tell him that instead of picking out a major I would be picking out baby names. Instead of watching college football games on Friday nights I would be watching my growing belly. And instead of bringing home a college degree I would be bringing home a newborn. I feared his reaction more than anything, and I wanted nothing more than to crawl into my twin bed beneath the Mariah Carey posters, close my eyes and wake up the next morning to find out it was all a dream.

I called my dad at work that morning and asked to meet him for lunch at his office. When we sat down at the tables outside his building, I took a deep breath and proceeded to break the news. I watched his face change from curiosity to sadness, as he listened intently to a story all too familiar. He didn't want me to face the same hardships as he had, struggling to raise a baby right out of high school.

My thoughts drifted to just a couple of years earlier - the many nights I watched him work on homework after serving us dinner, pushing himself to obtain his college degree that he put off so many years before. I told my dad that day that I would not let this ruin my life, no matter the difficult path ahead. And quite possibly I was convincing myself more so than my dad.

The following weeks were busy, as I packed up my entire life into a 1984 Pontiac Sunbird and kissed my dad goodbye. I drove the eighteen hours back to Texas, determined to be the best single mom to this unexpected gift. Upon arriving in Dallas, I was told the offer to live with my mom and her then husband no longer stood. She was 'not stable,' according to her husband, so my Sunbird remained full and we had nowhere to go. I was fortunate to have an incredibly generous aunt and uncle take me into their home and allow me to stay as long as necessary. I was thankful for their hospitality and called them my 'postcards from God' - arriving the day I needed them most.

I soon found a job at a local childcare facility, where I was able to work with babies and toddlers. I learned so much from the other teachers and caregivers, but more than anything I learned from my babies. From feeding them to diapering them, playing with them on the floor until my belly grew too large, and rocking them to sleep. I was prepared for my baby girl now, and so excited to meet the child who had already changed me and made me even more determined than ever.

Ariana was born on a beautiful Friday morning in May, just four months after finding out I was going to be a mom. She was perfect in every single way, and I fell in love with motherhood. I was able to move into a transition house the following month, an important step towards getting my own place. I formed some amazing friendships with other moms staying in the home, some from abusive situations or divorce. I was provided assistance with clothing, healthcare, childcare, and even groceries during my few months there.

I responded to an ad for a sales job in the classifieds section of the Dallas Morning News in November 1998 and prepared extensively for my interview. After several interviews and tests, I was offered a job with a major insurance company, working in sales at their regional office in Dallas. I was ecstatic because it meant I would have a steady paycheck as well as health insurance for the two of us. I sailed through the licensing and training program in record time, and was officially a licensed insurance agent! Within two months, I was in the top ten sales for the month, and finally I signed the lease on my first apartment. This was a huge accomplishment for me - and less than a year after my baby girl was born.

I didn't really care at the time that the apartment was only 500 square feet or that I slept on the floor next to Ariana's crib for the first month we lived there. I was just happy to have a place of our own, and I finally unpacked some of the boxes that originally traveled with me from my dad's house so many months ago. After a couple of paychecks, I was able to afford a cheap futon for the living room, which became my own make-shift bedroom that year. It's funny to admit it now, but I was so accustomed to moving every six months that I found it nearly impossible to renew a single apartment lease. Every time I called my dad to tell him I was moving, he laughed. Later he revealed he had only written my address in pencil in his address book after that first move.

I had so many goals at that time, but at the top of my list was being successful in my career, to give my daughter a stable life and home. I worked alongside some coworkers who had been sitting in the same cubicle with the same Plantronics over-the-ear headset for five or ten years, and they all seemed unfulfilled and unhappy. There was an unspoken 'shelf life' in a call center, and after two years of talking on the phone to what seemed like the entire US population, the thrill of seeing my name in the top sales no longer excited me. I left to work for another insurance company, this time in a busy store-front agency, with the opportunity to write additional insurance products and interact face-to-face with clients. I was eager to learn, and within a few years I was able to work as a 'floater', taking only short-term or temporary assignments with various agencies, filling in for vacationing agents or agents on medical leave, and even providing emergency relief during a catastrophe or other special circumstances. It was during this time that I finally allowed myself to date again, and I met someone new - my first real relationship since the pregnancy.

I married him two years later, and then my sweet daughter Mya was born during an ice storm in February, 2003. Even though I was certainly in a better position (financially) than when Ariana was born, my new baby girl's arrival only fueled my ambition to succeed even more. I wanted to teach both of my daughters how to persevere no matter what. After a few months of rest with my new baby, my next goal was in sight: to become an independent insurance agent. I was only 23 years old, but I knew I could do it now. I made the leap in 2004 to an independent agency, where I worked for a sole proprietor, and learned all the ins and outs of running an agency. A year later I was faced with a decision to get pregnant or risk not being able to have more children later. We welcomed a son, Joshua, in October of 2005. Our nine-pound bundle of joy, paired with my prior female medical struggles, caused some complications during labor. Both of us were fine, but I endured a few years of pain and issues after his birth. This led to a full hysterectomy before the age of 30.

When I returned to work after the surgery, my mother offered to keep the kids that first week, being it was the last couple weeks of summer. School would be starting later that month, and it gave me a chance to adjust to returning to work full-time. During that week, my mother had some sort of breakdown, which caused her to sever the pigtail braids right off of Mya, who was only 6 years old at the time. I remember flying down the Dallas North Tollway in my car, trying to see through a flood of tears, desperately hoping my mother would not physically harm my children in the thirty-minute drive. When I arrived, I was devastated to see the damage, but thankful that I could scoop up all three of my babies and run. We took Mya that next day to have her hair cut into an adorable short bob, and we talked with her every day to make sure she was okay after the incident. From that moment on, I limited contact with my mother. We were conveniently busy when she wanted to get together, and I didn't call her to 'just talk' anymore. I had always known she had a dark side that comes out at times, but I never thought she would do anything to my kids.

The next few years I worked incredibly hard in my position, rising into management and becoming a high net-worth insurance specialist for individuals and families, as well as celebrity risk. I began coaching a fast-pitch softball team at Ariana's request, and quickly was promoted to join the board of the non-profit softball league. Eventually I ran for President, faced with enormous challenges as the first female in the position in more than ten years. It wasn't easy, but I knew my purpose was greater than the obstacles I had faced. I loved my newfound calling to help guide the teenage girls who played for me, along with those who supported me on the board. We worked countless hours designing a new website, developing the social media aspects, and taking the league's paper registration online. After serving alongside such hard working volunteers, I now see nonprofit organizations and volunteer groups in a new light.

Why did you want to start this business? When did you know you were meant to launch your own business?

It was during my time on this non-profit board that I knew I needed to launch my photography business. I had begun shooting pictures for the softball league and friends, and the emotions my images invoked are the reason I pursued the business. My photography is artistic and interpretive, which I felt was unique to the industry.

During this time I also felt compelled to share another gift - my voice - with the world. So I began singing at weddings, corporate events, parties, and even singing telegrams. I called my business "Black Tie Ballads," and though I didn't become famous or a YouTube sensation, I was incredibly fulfilled. One of my favorite moments included singing 'When You Say Nothing At All' a Capella for a wedding at the new Dallas Cowboys Stadium, on the star in the center of the field. I also remember singing 'Happy Birthday' for a special lady at a nursing home in Fort Worth, Texas. Her son found my ad online and asked me to sing to her on her 91st birthday. She was so humbled by his gift, and told me in all of her 91 years on this Earth, she had never been sung to before. I received a standing ovation from everyone in the nursing home, and hugs from all of the family and nurses. I was also honored to sing at a friend's wedding, as well as several weddings for folks I'd never known before.

In 2011, I was given the opportunity to build my own client book for a New York based insurance agency, and the ability to have full ownership of my book. Though I wasn't able to have equity ownership in the agency, to own the client book was a huge advantage, especially in the world of insurance, which is filled with ironclad employment agreements and costly non-compete contracts.

So I left my leadership position with steep goals to build an impressive client base of customers that I would be able to retain for the duration of my career. This new position would also allow me to spend more time with my family, and the location was only a few miles from my home, which eliminated my hour long commute each day. I was also able to finally launch my photography business, Janet Campbell Photography. I was still learning and honing my craft, but I was determined to capture something the world had not yet seen before. I didn't advertise my business at first; perhaps I was intimidated by some of my friends who were amazing photographers. I finally received some advice from a stranger I had met at a photography class, and his words changed my outlook altogether. He told me "there will always be other photographers out there, and many of them will amaze you with their images. But keep in mind the world needs all of us to share our view from our own lens, even if it's just to move one single soul." His words touched me, and I stopped comparing myself to other photographers.

What has being in business for yourself done for you?

Being in business for myself has taught me the true value of my time, and how fulfilling life can be when you are following your dreams and not just dreaming about them.

In March 2011, the month I began my new job, my grandmother unexpectedly passed away. I took a few days off to attend her wake, and I sang a hymn, "Precious Lord, Take My Hand" at her funeral to honor her memory. That same month my husband and I separated, just weeks before our eighth wedding anniversary. It was a sad time, but I could not let myself give in to the feelings of failure or regret. I was determined to overcome this obstacle, the same as the obstacles in my past. So 2011 was the start of another chapter in my life, now a single mom of three kids. That same year I found out that Ariana's birth father had passed away. He had no relationship with Ariana prior to his death, so no real sadness overcame either of us; but perhaps a form of closure now, just ten years after he had terminated his parental rights.

The rest of that year passed by quickly, as did the many challenges of being a single mom (again). It was now the spring of 2012, and my client book was slowly growing and building. I was still coaching Ariana's softball team, and many of the players had been with me since the first season in 2008. After the closing ceremonies of the spring season, many of my players left to join tournament teams and high school softball teams, and I had to (reluctantly) say goodbye to our team. We enjoyed a few weeks off that summer, but Ariana then began to drop hints of wishing we could form a new team. The week of her first week as a freshman in high school, we held tryouts for a new team, though we weren't sure the plan for the team just yet. The girls were too old to play in our recreational league, so this could potential be a tournament team (though an inexperienced one!)

A coach from our former league, Harry Bernstein, had coached an opposing team for the past three years, and he showed up for the tryouts with his daughter, Livia. She was a great softball player, tall, and very excited to play again. I invited her dad to coach alongside me, and he graciously accepted. I wasn't too sure of his coaching style, but he seemed eager to help, so I welcomed him to the team. After a couple of weeks of practices, I invited him out for a meeting to discuss plans for the team, and we met at a restaurant in town one evening. We discussed softball for a bit, but then somehow we covered everything from kids to marriage to divorce...and eventually the restaurant was closing for the evening. The next day, he sent me a text and invited me on a real date. I said yes, of course, and anxiously awaited that Saturday night. The same day as our perfect date, I also completed my first bridal portrait session. I was so eager to get home and edit the photos that I almost cancelled my date that evening with Harry. I'm so glad I didn't cancel, because it was the best first date of my life.

That fall, a long-time insurance client contacted me regarding a friend of his who was interested in talking with me about an opportunity. This industry legend, Brook Crawford, was building a new insurance agency in Dallas, and looking to grow at record pace in the coming years. He did not, at the time, have an opening for me - but we agreed to keep in touch, should the timing work out later. Over the next several months, my mother had some medical issues related to her mental illness. She was hospitalized multiple times, and struggled to obtain a job or maintain her home. I stepped in and helped as much as possible, agreeing to act as power of attorney and negotiate with her landlord and doctors, but eventually her refusal to take her medication only strained our relationship. In March, after several weeks of manic symptoms, I tried to accompany her to her psychiatrist's visit to advise him she was not taking her medication. She then screamed at me in a full waiting room, 'I hate you little girl, and I wish you had never been born!' I tried to hold back my tears, telling myself it was her illness talking and not really her, but when I left that medical plaza that day, I knew I needed to break away from her to protect myself and my family. That cold day in March was the last time I ever saw my mother. I've heard through family members that she lost her home, but was living with a relative, and I do think of her often and hope she is seeking the help she so desperately needs.

The following June, Brook Crawford's new agency, AmeriCap Insurance Group, was merging with another agency and my experience was needed. I was offered the role of Vice President of Personal Lines, but I was also offered the position of Partner, the youngest at only age 33. Finally I had attained the goal! I was able to bring all of my loyal clients with me, and begin to build a foundation with a group of partners I greatly respected and admired. That next month, Harry proposed and we announced our engagement. My photography business also began to grow, as I booked my first wedding. My hard work was beginning to pay off, and we renamed the business CampStein Photography - which was a combination of my former last name (Campbell) and my soon-to-be-married last name (Bernstein).

In January 2014, I attended a seminar in Austin for leadership, and came back to the office with a new list of goals for the agency. I wanted to redesign our website and begin to utilize social media, which had not been done before. My partners were a little skeptical, but they allowed me the freedom to experiment with different strategies over the next several months. After consistent effort, the agency's online presence increased, as did the referrals. I was then given an additional role of Social Media Director, which led to additional projects for marketing materials such as direct mailers and custom designed campaigns. I never knew how to create graphics or marketing pieces before, but I learned quickly and fell in love with design. I began to combine my photography skills with design, which opened new doors.

If someone asked you, who are your ideal clients, what would you say?

My ideal client is someone who knows that photography is a form of art, and not just a person with a camera. It is someone who has something to say to the world, and needs an artist to expose it for them. A very good friend of mine was being interviewed for a magazine article, and was contacted by the reporter to coordinate her story and schedule photos with their magazine photographer. My friend dismissed the offer for their photographer, and stated 'no thanks; I have my own photographer!' She called me moments after and said she needed photos and quickly, and I dropped everything to make it happen. One of my images of her was actually chosen for the cover of the magazine, and they used several others in a multiple-page spread for the article. CampStein Photography was now published! These are the types of clients I value above all others, for they are my biggest fans and supporters. I make it a point to personally get to know each of my clients - beyond the traditional 'where are you from?' type questions.

Soon after my magazine cover, I received information that I was nominated for a magazine, 'Women of Distinction', and I was interviewed for the article. After I completed the interview and submitted the photos, I felt compelled to give back and help other women feel as honored as I. In May 2014, I created a blog called www.BeyondHerImage.com, where I planned to photograph women of integrity and profile them on my blog and social media channels, while sharing their story. I wasn't certain of the goals for the blog, but I knew I had to do this for women. This was part of my purpose. Photographing and interviewing my first few women for the blog was exciting, but writing and sharing their stories was liberating! I had no agenda, no product to sell, and no ulterior motive, other than to promote these amazing women. I used my gifts of photography and writing to bring stories to light that otherwise might not have been shared. One of my favorites of the blog posts was the story of a farmer, and why she chose the exhausting life of farming and homeschooling. I still reflect upon that post often, as her words are relevant to the struggles we all face as women, juggling careers and kids, along with our passions – despite the pressures of society to conform. I am often asked if I plan to 'quit' my job as an Insurance Risk Advisor to become a photographer full-time. I can honestly say that I love my purpose as an advisor, and I feel truly honored to have two successful businesses that fulfill my desire to serve others and share my passion with the world.

What is your most rewarding experience since starting your own business?

My most rewarding moment was being asked by the Independent Insurance Agents of Dallas (IIAD) to photograph their All Industry Day in November 2014. As an insurance agent, I've been a member of the organization for many years, and to be asked to photograph my fellow peers and industry professionals was truly an honor.

What must have resources would you recommend to use in your business?

I recommend anyone in business hire a business coach. I also recommend surrounding yourself with a support network of folks who care about you, and who can help you with things like website design, social media, marketing, photography, and just listening when you need to vent.

What is the biggest obstacle you've encountered since being in business? How did you overcome it?

My biggest challenge in my photography business has been communicating my fee for sessions. Potential clients would call and inquire about booking, and once I would mention my fee, they'd thank me and never call back. After meeting with my business coach, Butch Bellah, he was able to help me establish a 'script' of sorts, breaking down my process and communicating to potential clients what's involved in a session, from the shooting to editing, and effectively putting a value on my time. Once I figured out how to do this, I was much more comfortable and booked more sessions.

One of the biggest struggles women entrepreneurs have is how to price themselves. What advice would you share about pricing your services and offerings?

Once I figured out how to tell potential clients what I charged, what helped me most was writing down a fee for every service I offered, and included the number of hours estimated for each service.

How do you measure success and what is your definition of success?

Success to me is feeling fulfilled while photographing, knowing I'm earning the fee I need to sustain the business, and having the financial freedom to donate my time and services when needed.

What have you learned about yourself in running your business?

I've learned that I'm a lot more disciplined than I ever gave myself credit for, and that my hard work ethic has only helped me become more successful. I'm so dedicated to delivering amazing customer service that many nights I'm up until 2am editing photos! I've also learned that I could easily become a workaholic if I didn't balance my schedule responsibly.

What 3 things do you now wish you would've known when you started?

I do admit that owning your own business certainly has a learning curve, but I wish I would have known early on that it was okay to say no, and that I didn't have to photograph everyone and everything that came along. I've since found that I don't enjoy the traditional 'head shots' that so many photographers offer. Standing someone in front of a green screen and manipulating them into contrived poses just doesn't fulfill me, and I'm never satisfied with the final product, no matter how much editing I do. I've stopped offering those types of sessions, and I feel so much better about staying true to my style and being authentic. I have no problem referring potential clients to other photographers who may be more suited to their needs.

In November 2014, Harry Bernstein and I were married in an interfaith ceremony, in which we celebrated our love under a Chuppah, in front of a para-rabbi, a minister, and all of our family and friends. It was a beautiful night, full of laughter and tears, though mostly tears of joy. My only sadness was that my mother was not able to be a part of this special day. I was incredibly blessed by my stepmother, Tammy Scott, and my mother-in-law, Shelley Bernstein, who both stepped in and supported me in all the ways that I needed that day. My oldest daughters, Ariana and Livia, both amazed me with their willingness to help that day, both of them running around the venue doing last minute things to make sure our day was perfect. Our younger daughters, Mya and Sofia, brought me such joy as they embraced the emotions and excitement of the day. And my new sister, Dana Sherman, who accepted me the first moment we spoke on the phone, was by my side the entire day to help, or provide comic relief when chaos ensued! I will forever remember being surrounded by all of them as they helped me into my wedding gown. In that moment, all of the trials and tribulations throughout my childhood and adulthood began to scroll through my head, as I realized how thankful I truly was for the happiness that had finally come my way.

That evening, during the wedding reception, my nine year-old son, Joshua, asked me to take a photo with him in the photo booth. He grabbed me by the hand and we skipped through the venue to the photo booth, only to find the vendor was already packing up for the evening. Josh was defeated, and I could see he wanted to cry, but was trying so hard to be strong. I quickly told him to run and grab some photo booth props and I flagged down the photographer. When Josh came back, we made our own make-shift photo booth, and our photographer snapped some pictures of us, as we giggled and posed for the camera. After we were done taking the photos, I hugged Josh and told him, 'never let anyone tell you something can't be done. There's always a way.' He smiled at me, squinting his eyes a bit to tell me he wasn't quite sure my comment only applied to the photo booth fiasco. But I knew I had planted the seed...the seed of perseverance.

How do you keep yourself motivated and encouraged when things don't go right?

My husband is my biggest supporter, and when things are off track, I reach out to him. I am harder on myself than anyone else, and I struggle with being a perfectionist at times. Harry has the ability to remind me of all the wonderful things I've accomplished, which I tend to forget when I'm under stress.

What's your biggest business goal over the next 12 months, and what will you do to meet it?

My biggest business goal for the next 12 months is to double the number of photo sessions I did the prior year, and I intend to utilize social media and referrals to accomplish my goal. I also want to take Beyond Her Image to a larger audience, using my photography and writing talents to potentially touch thousands of lives.

What makes you a Woman That Impacts? How are you impacting your world?

I empower everyone around me, no matter the environment, to pursue their dreams and become whatever they desire most. My biggest impact is probably going to be through my blog, BeyondHerImage.com, where I share so many amazing stories of women of integrity, promoting them through my Facebook pages, LinkedIn feeds, Twitter and Instagram.

Continue the Conversation with Janet Bernstein:

Janet Bernstein built her business, CampStein Photography, while successfully managing her career as an Insurance Risk Advisor, Social Media Director and Vice President of Personal Insurance for AmeriCap Insurance Group, where she is a partner. She has two booming businesses, and embraces the challenges of juggling a blended family and work. She resides in Carrollton, Texas with her husband, Harold Bernstein and their five children: Ariana, Livia, Mya, Sofia and Joshua.

Below are the various ways that you can connect with Janet and learn more about what she has to offer.

Website:
www.campsteinphotography.com

Twitter:
www.twitter.com/CampSteinPhoto

Facebook:
www.facebook.com/campsteinphography

MELYNDA LILLY
Executive Consultant, Ambit Energy

Tell us a little about yourself. We want to learn about the person behind the brand.

I'm happy to have been married to my high school sweetheart, Mark Lilly, for 33 years and blessed to have three grown children (Keith, 30; Krista, 28; Chad, 26), an awesome son-in-law, Travis, & daughter-in-law, Kristin. I'm amazed to have six grandchildren: Gavyn, Ethan, Landon, Chase, Taylor and Peyton.

Our life revolves around our family. We spend all of our time together attending grandkids' sporting events including baseball, football, volleyball, basketball, cheerleading & gymnastics. I love the outdoors - especially water - boating, swimming, etc. Traveling with family and friends to see the beaches of the world has been my passion. I love people and welcome the building of relationships with people from all walks of life. There is always a reason to celebrate life. I celebrate every holiday and every birthday. Life is a celebration!

I love to read motivational books and attend personal growth & development seminars. I was very blessed to have a great coach and mentor, Jan Ruhe. She taught me that when the student is ready the teacher will appear. So at the young age of 26, I became an avid student of personal growth and development.

I have had many great teachers and coaches in my life, including Tom Hopkins, Jim Rohn, Tony Robbins, Tom "Big Al" Schreiter, Ira Gedan, John Kalench, John Maxwell, Darren Hardy, Zig Ziglar, Og Madino, Dr. Tom Barrett, Andy Andrews, Eric Worre, Dani Johnson, Caterina Rando, Esther Spina and countless more! I thank them all for the wisdom they poured into their books. All the live seminars were life-changing events. The best advice I can give is to never ever stop learning; continue on your journey of personal growth and development for a lifetime.

I am truly blessed with exceptional parents, Rex & Charlotte Powell, who role modeled unconditional love. My parents have been married 54 years. They have been very involved in our lives, never missing a birth of seven grandchildren and seven great grandchildren. They attended every event of their grandchildren over the years. So I am blessed to have great role models for parents.

My dad was also an entrepreneur. He always told me that if you are going to work hard you might as well work hard for yourself. So glad I followed in his footsteps!

God truly blessed me when he found me the man of my dreams, Mark Lilly. Yes, we were high school sweethearts. We started dating my sophomore year in high school. I graduated high school in May 1981, and we got married June 6th, 1981. Our life has truly been a fairy tale! Mark has always treated me like a princess! He is the most amazing care taker - always putting others needs before his own. He continues to be very involved in our kids' lives and super involved in our grand kids' lives.

Mark was diagnosed with MS at the very young age of 34. I have watched him deal with his disease over the years. What I have learned from Mark is his attitude to never give in or give up! Most people would never know Mark has MS because he never complains and always pushes through to attend everything he can that deals with family & friends!

Mark is my biggest supporter and cheers me on in everything I do. The stress of not having to worry about money is a big burden off of him. Our motto is to live each day like it is your last! Live a life with no regrets, attend everything, and make time for what's important. We love making unforgettable memories together with our family, friends, and business partners!

Share with us what your business is and why you wanted to start this business.

I help people save money and make money on a daily basis with my energy business. I have been in the direct selling industry for over 26 years. Before Ambit Energy, I was in the toy business for 20 years. When I was invited to become a business partner with Ambit Energy, the concept that there was no inventory, no deliveries, and no collections greatly appealed to me.

Once I enrolled with Ambit Energy every month when my customers paid their electric bill, I get paid a portion of that bill creating a residual income. I get paid month after month after month. I loved the fact that I help people save money on a bill they must pay every month. I have helped hundreds of people eliminate their electric bill with Ambit's FREE energy program.

Since Ambit is a family business, I leave a legacy to my grandchildren and future grandchildren for generations to come. My business is a generational wealth building business and that makes me happy - 99.9% of my time is invested in helping people make money with Ambit Energy.

I love changing a person's financial future for the better. My reason for starting this business is simple: To help average people earn an above average income so they can do things in life they are passionate about! I love the fact that I don't sell a product. I don't have to convince anyone to try my product or try to fit it into their monthly budget. Everyone has already budgeted for their electricity bill. I just help them lower that bill or even get it for free.

Ambit's product is a public utility that is unconsciously purchased & habitually used. We deliver the product to the consumer at below retail with the benefits that everybody already uses it and understands it. As a representative, I don't collect money, and I don't change the way the consumer buys the product. Electricity is the perfect auto ship. We don't have to sell anything. We are in the education business.   There are three things energy companies need to do right to gather & maintain loyal customers: 1) have a competitive price 2) good customer service and 3) great customer benefits.

Ambit has some of the best customer benefits in the industry. Every customer who chooses Ambit as their electricity provider receives a 3- day, 2-night weekend getaway just for trying the service. Good in over 25 cities across the United States. We have a satisfaction guarantee that if anything should happen during the switching process, Ambit will pay their first month's electric bill. We also have a monthly travel rewards program.

As soon as a customer is energized with Ambit we give them 2000 points. Every month the kWh usage is added as points to the travel program. Over time, as your point value increases month after month, you can trade in your points for different vacation packages. How would you like to go to a spa or golf getaway, escape to the Bahamas, Mexico, Dominican Republic, or maybe a cruise? All this is possible just for paying your electric bill each and every month.

Now you are rewarded for paying a bill you have to pay no matter what. All of our customers also receive a FREE website so they can refer their friends and family to Ambit. Once a customer has referred 15 customers, Ambit will take the average of those 15 customers' electric bills and apply that energy credit to their bill. As long as the customer maintains 15 referral customers, they will receive their free energy credit every single month.

I have personally saved over $10,000 in free energy with Ambit's FREE energy program. I love the benefits of owning my own business - flexible schedule, tax benefits and the power of unlimited income potential. Every year my income has increased with Ambit - some years it has doubled and even tripled. Being an employee of someone else, this type of yearly income increase would never have happened. We do two simple things with Ambit: 1) gather a handful of loyal customers, the people we know, love and trust and 2) help others do the same.

When did you know you were meant to launch your own business?

When I met with the co-founders of Ambit Energy, Jere Thompson Jr. & Chris Chambless, I was convinced they would build a billion-dollar business. I was not going to miss the boat on this opportunity. So, I got happily involved and went to work. I knew if I worked 10 to 15 years in this business, I would be leaving a legacy for my family.

When I started with Ambit, I was committed to build this business for as long as it took. There is a day you get into network marketing, but nothing happens until network marketing gets into you. For the first two years I worked Ambit along with my other business. Ambit Energy did become a billion dollar company in seven years with over one million customers. I am very grateful that I made the decision to start my own Ambit Energy business.

What has being in business for yourself done for you?

I have complete time freedom and financial freedom. I wake up when I am done sleeping - no alarm clocks in my house! I decide every day whether to work or play. I love Ambit Energy because we have been able to achieve financial freedom. All our bills are paid each and every month with residual income whether I work or not. Our full-time job is spending time with family. I love getting to work with my family and the idea that all their dreams will come true. I would have to say the personal growth & development. What I have learned from being an entrepreneur has been my greatest accomplishment. I am so honored to have been asked to write a chapter in Behind Her Brand. I am also currently writing a book with my good friend and business partner, Alice Hinckley. Our book will be about Lifetime Relationships and will be released in the spring of 2015.   I believe all these opportunities are available to me because I embraced the courage to be my own boss and learn the skills I needed to succeed in network marketing.

If someone asked you, who are your ideal clients, what would you say?

I would say everyone because everyone uses electricity--24 hours a day, seven days a week! It's the perfect product! I do two very simple things: 1) help people make money and 2) save money. In this economy today that is exactly what people are looking to do - save money and make money. Helping people become financially free is awesome, but helping them to have time freedom is priceless. In the world today people either have lots of money but no time, or lots of time but no money.

So I love helping people achieve financial freedom and time freedom. So my ideal client would be anyone who uses electricity and for those looking to buy back their time.

How do you measure success and what is your definition of success?

I learned from Tom Hopkins almost 25 years ago: "Success is the continuous journey towards the achievement of pre-determined, worthwhile goals." So I set goals in all areas of my life: health, finance, relationships and personal growth. Success is an everyday job.

Once you achieve one goal, you must always have the next goal ready to be working towards. As long as I am staying consistent & persistent towards my goals, I am successful. Success is measured by how many times one can fail and try again. Never give up or never quit, and you will succeed. To me, success is adding value to my company, but also to my overall life and the lives of other people.

What was the biggest obstacle you've encountered since being in business? How did you overcome it?

It had been learning to work with people who deserve my time and not the people who need it. I so desperately wanted people to be successful. I would go out of my way to help them, but they would always have excuses why they could not do something. I have learned to say at the very beginning with a new team member, "My efforts will match your efforts. I will work as hard for you in your business as you are willing to work yourself." Now I do not feel guilty if the person is not successful because they did not put any effort into their business. I have also been learning to prioritize my time. It's easy to get caught up in busy- work, email, social media, etc. Last year a business partner and I sent each other our weekly to do list of all our goals for the week, and then we would have a 30 minute phone call on Monday mornings. On that call we would talk about what we did accomplish from the previous week and our action plan for the current week. Having the weekly goals all written out and being able to check them off during the week really helped me to stay focused.

What have you learned about yourself in running your business?

Communication is one of the keys to success. You must stay in touch with your leaders, your team, your customers, and your prospects. If you stay focused on the goal, you will get there! Be the leader and people will follow you. Don't listen to the naysayers--align yourself with positive people. Have a clear vision of what you want and where you are going. I will not allow anyone to steal my dream. I will control my destiny. I will persist until I succeed. Treat people the way you want to be treated. Every person you meet, look at them as if they had a stamp on their forehead that said "MAKE ME FEEL IMPORTANT!" I am in the people business and energy just happens to be my service. Ninety percent of my success depends on my attitude. Therefore, I must always attend self-improvement seminars as a huge part of my success.

What was your most rewarding experience since starting your own business?

I have had several rewarding experiences, I will share a few. When my youngest son, Chad Lilly, became financially free at the age of 23 years old. He graduated college and never had to submit a resume. He joined my team during my first 6 months in business. Chad worked his Ambit business part-time alongside being a full-time college student. By the time Chad graduated college, his residual income from Ambit Energy paid all his bills.

Chad's life today: He is married and gets to pursue his passion in the music industry. He still builds his Ambit business part-time, and his residual income continues to grow year after year!   I got promoted to Executive Consultant and my team threw a surprise party for me; the CMO, Chris Chambless, came to the party to congratulate my team on our promotion. I earned over $100,000 a year working part time from home. I was on the cover of the *Success from Home* magazine in 2011 & 2012 and had my profile story in the *Success from Home* magazine in 2014. I feel so truly blessed to have had all these experiences with my company, Ambit Energy.

What 3 things do you now wish you would've known when you started?

1.) Talk less, listen more! Find out what the person wants and needs in their life and show them how they can achieve it! God gave you two ears and only one mouth. Hmm, something to think about...

2.) Keep it simple! Never do anything other people can't copy. People need to follow in your footsteps. If you make it complicated, you will lose people along the way.

3.) Believe in yourself. Believe more in your dreams than your doubts. Don't settle for anything but the best that life has to offer.

How do you keep yourself motivated and encouraged when things don't go right?

I read motivational books as well as listen to great up-beat music and motivational tapes. Stay plugged into positive people who lift you up and not drag you down. Get a massage or facial. I take a walk. I avoid conflict. I detach myself from negative people. Read, Read, Read! Readers are leaders, and leaders are readers!

What's your biggest business goal over the next 12 months and what will you do to meet it?

Help three people on my team promote to Executive Consultant which is an enormous step in our business. Help them develop a plan of action and stay focused on the goal. Personally add 30 new consultants. A 2015 challenge with my team will be The Hall of Fame Club. Everyone who personally sponsors 15 people and helps 5 team members is promoted up the compensation plan. All winners will be treated to a VIP 5 event in December 2015. Publishing *Lifetime Relationship* book with my co-author, Alice Hinckley by March 2015.

What advice would you give to a woman entrepreneur who is ready to take her business to the next level?

Believe you can become wealthy! You are worthy of wealth! Three B's to Success: 1) Believe in yourself 2) Believe in your product and 3) Believe in your company. Build great relationships with people. We all do business with people we know, like & trust. Also get a coach, someone who will keep you accountable and challenge you. Find a mentor and do what they do; read what they read.

Make a list of what you are willing to work for. Work on yourself. Attend more seminars. Give yourself permission to succeed. Write down all your goals. Read: *The Greatest Salesman in the World* by OG Mandino and *Think and Grow Rich* by Napoleon Hill. Take care of yourself first and DREAM big! Just decide, to decide to go for greatness and make it happen! Step outside your comfort zone and take a risk! You will never know until you try!

One of the biggest struggles women entrepreneurs have is how to price themselves. What advice would you share about pricing your services and offerings?

My business is not about pricing. We have no control over the price of energy. That is the best part of being the CEO of my own energy distribution business. Our owners are in the energy part of the business. They set the prices of energy and open new markets. I just gather the customers and build a team of consultants.

What must have resources would you recommend to use in your business?

In my business, everyone needs their own personal website to run their business. You subscribe to the website with Ambit Energy for $26 a month. We run our entire business with this website. Glad to say that $26 a month is a very low overhead to run a business.

My company Ambit Energy has also been featured in *Success from Home* magazine the last five years. These magazines are one of the Best Business Tools to show the Ambit success stories and potential opportunity. The Direct Selling News Global 100 lists all the top 100 MLM companies in the world and their rank. Ambit Energy was ranked #12 in 2014.

Just released is a new DVD called "Rise of the Entrepreneur." This documentary film is excellent for those considering becoming a network marketing professional. Start building your library of self-help books.

"There are three things to leave behind: your photographs, your library and your personal journals. These

things are certainly going to be more valuable to future generations than your furniture!" Jim Rohn

What makes you a Woman That Impacts? How are you impacting your world?

My desire is to mentor, inspire and empower other men & women. I have been truly blessed to have some great mentors & teachers in my life. They believed in me and taught me to work harder on myself to develop the skills I needed to build a business. I am honored to pay it forward to help others be the best they can be and live the life they deserve. I am very involved in my community, helping small business owners connect with people in the community.

Our group is called Connect! In Keller. I also help lead a leads referral group In Keller, Texas, Leading Edge Referrals which also helps small business owners in the community. I have also been involved in the Ambit-ious Women's Conference (AWC) the last five years by being on the women's council helping plan the event.

AWC has grown from 75 women to over 1000 women who come for a weekend to get inspired & empowered to build their business and go for greatness in everything they do!

Make a point to engage in random acts of kindness. It makes you feel good and the person feel good. It's a win win! Be Generous! There are 6 ways to be generous. You can give someone your time, your listening, your money, words of appreciation or encouragement and gifts. When I can make a difference in someone's life for the better, then I know it will impact the world, because they can go out and do the same for someone else.

Continue the Conversation with Melynda Lilly:

Melynda Lilly, Executive Consultant with Ambit Energy, embraces the freedom network marketing has brought to her life to focus on family and travel. During her 26 years in direct sales & marketing, Melynda has built large organizations helping average people earn an above average income so they can do the things in life they are passionate about.

Melynda is incredibly passionate about her family which includes her supportive husband, Mark, three grown children, and six beautiful grandchildren.

Below are the various ways that you can connect with Melynda and learn more about what she has to offer.

Website:

www.lilly.energygoldrush.com

Twitter:

www.twitter.com/ Mklilly

Facebook:

www.facebook.com/melyndalilly

www.facebook.com/ambitwithmelynda

LARISSA RUBIJEVSKY
Your Realtor For Life

Tell us a little about yourself. We want to learn about the person behind the brand.

My family and I fled post-Communist Russia in 1994– "Perestroika" times, if you recall. The country had fallen into the hands of criminals, and a heaving mass of angry, lost, chronically depressed and scared people tried their best to survive in the aftermath. The whole system was built on the suppression of your initiative, desires, creativity and drive. There was no room for an open mind, ambition, entrepreneurship...

It was clear that my country could no longer be my home. So there I was, almost 30, stepping off the plane, with my completely dysfunctional luggage in tow. I was terrified of the idea of rebuilding my life from the rubble of the past.

My English was horrible, I had an education but no marketable skills, and I had only a vague understanding of how this country worked. I had yet to understand its values, traditions, culture, work, even its money. Lost doesn't even begin to describe how I felt as I took my first steps onto foreign soil. It was like jumping off a cliff into a churning sea. But you know that giddy feeling you get in your stomach just as you are about to dive in? I felt it that day. Just under the terrified surface was a swirling pool of happiness. Deep down inside, I believed that this was the country of opportunity and even little insignificant me had a fighting chance.

Then came the cultural shock — the people of America! I was positive that aliens or gods were walking the streets here. I was used to cynics and negativity; Americans were the total opposite of what I came from.

They were beautiful, friendly, honest and free! And above all, they felt like humans. I was in comparison euphoria and seriously was ready to hug and kiss every person I met. I loved my new life and where the Universe put me. I felt so excited, privileged and happy to be part of this "Mount Olympus" community and at the same time determined to be worthy of such company. I can smile now as I look back at my naïveté, but my admiration was sincere. It was the huge contrast with the past that helped me to expand my mind, quiet my fears, and perform at my best ability.

Scaling the godly mountain was not easy. I worked multiple jobs, long hours and went to school at the same time. I looked around, I listened, I learned, I made mistakes, I cried, I learned again, and I continued to believe that I came here for a reason. I was creating new life for my family and myself and in the process I created a new me, one that recognized that I was capable of more than I had ever dreamed of. My mind was sharper, my heart fuller - every day since it has been a wonder and an opportunity for growth that I cling to with all my might.

Share with us what your business is and why you wanted to start this business.

The reality was I didn't want to start anything of my own. Yes, I wasn't perfectly happy with my 9-to-5 job. Yes, I was tired and frustrated at times. Yes, I knew I had little potential for growth, but we had **stability**! My husband, a computer programmer made very decent salary. We bought a nice house in a great area. We saved money, never wanted for anything, and could take vacations twice a year. After all the struggle and hard work, life was finally good and even better than I expected. I leaned back and breathed a sigh of relief... Ahhhh...

Then the spousal nagging came along. My husband kept bugging, bugging and bugging me about how much more I could do and accomplish running my own business. He had a pet idea of realtors making great money while enjoying full independence. Being a mathematician and a computing wizard, he quickly projected that I just had to sell four or five houses a year to double my income, work my own hours and not have to experience the bone-aching exhaustion. Maybe there was some bias here, but he thought people liked me and in his mind that was already half the battle. I finally gave up and decided to try just to get him off my neck. I got my license and started working for ReMax Palos Verdes, the largest real estate company in my area. Oh, boy... In real estate sales, you recognize very quickly that those beautiful Olympians walking up your streets might turn into the ugliest demons, and that they might be your clients, neighbors and peers! Ouch!

What has being in business for yourself done for you?

Once I started on my own, without the comfort of a guaranteed paycheck and benefits, first I wanted to kill my husband a few times for pushing me into this change and new turmoil. Dude was lucky he was still alive after he made me go through another, even more intense hellscape of self-doubt, fear and frustration. Nothing was right in the beginning. I wanted to quit every time I saw a client walking away from me, another agent openly laughing at me, or my family left alone every single weekend. Where was the independence, the freedom? However, either my natural Russian stubbornness took over or I stopped caring about the rejection, but something made me clench my teeth and go on. And eventually the money came in, and then the benefits, and at last the satisfaction of a job well done.

If someone asked you, who are your ideal clients, what would you say?

There is no such thing as an ideal client in real estate sales. I'm sorry to say it, but that's brutal reality. Considering the super competitive nature of the business, always-changing market and technology you have to prove yourself as a true professional over and over again, even with past clients and referrals.

You must always reassert your worthiness, creativity, expertise, enthusiasm and full commitment to your **clients'** interests, not to your commission check. But once you prove it and trust is established and re-established, the real fun begins and that's my favorite part!

How do you measure success and what is your definition of success?

Success for me is all in two simple words - **Disciplined Mind.** If you master these two words, the world is yours!

I'm sure it never comes easy to any entrepreneur, especially us women with our natural multitasking tendencies. However a disciplined mind is the root of all success and I truly believe in it. I played competitive sports for years, so focus and discipline were second nature to me. That being said, maintaining the same mindset when you are your own boss means you've got to religiously follow it, re-assess it and constantly improve it. It is always work in progress. And that's ok!

The fact that we're even talking about it right now puts us into a very special category, women-entrepreneurs who stay above the ordinary crowd. The fact is that you, my dear, who's reading this right now, have stumbled across something very special, something that 90% of others don't get or have. YOU eventually attracted it through your thinking (or sub-thinking?). So acknowledge the power of your will and drive! With it, you can accomplish anything and make lots of money out of it, too!

What was the biggest obstacle you've encountered since being in business? How did you overcome it?

Oy vey, where do I start...

1.) My biggest and worst enemy was fear. I feared that there was always somebody smarter, more experienced, more creative, more articulate, and resourceful, you name it. They were tall, they were male, and they were NOT legally blonde, whatever... I still try very hard to consciously make myself stop right there, because this crap is only in my head. I have a special strategy for dealing with my fears - maybe it'll work for you too. First, I acknowledge it, picture it and shrink it ten times in imaginary size. Then, I put a clown's nose on it and give it a squeaky little Mickey Mouse voice. Turn your fear into some comical thing, make fun of it. Helps!

2.) My foreigner accent didn't help much, either. Of course, it's much better now, but in the beginning... you don't want to know. Think of your MBA Real Estate Consultant saying "asshole" instead of "hassle," and tons of other embarrassing things like that. Some people smiled and think it was cute. Some raised their brows and walked away. But just recently I realized that there's advantage in it because it's *different*. Not threatening or stupid. Different! So when I still do some small pronunciation "boo-boos", I just giggle and apologize and the reaction is always friendly. I'm working what I got, baby!

3.) Complacency is an inviting option, but I have always fought against it. After evaluating your position in your business, you need to be ready for constant work and improvement. How can I do it better? What did I learn last time? How can I be more creative? No matter how well I do, I know I can dream even bigger because limits, like my fears, are only in my head. There will be always people who try to talk you out of your vision. You absolutely MUST divorce that dynamic. Negativity as self-doubt can only drag you down. I'm sure you're tired of hearing this, but it's a necessary reminder! Positivity is key. Invite it into your life, and the rest will be easier to bear.

4.) The early failures. Oh dear... There were quite a few! I lost clients. I lost respect for people that I once trusted. I lost patience. I lost time and money doing unproductive marketing, prospecting or socializing. But guess what? Failures are good! I love each one of them because I learned a lot from them. You assess, re-evaluate and leave your past in the past without taking it personally or dwelling on it. Then out loud you say "Next!" and repeat it again and again.

You move on to the next level, next client, next experience, and next accomplishment but with new wisdom. From the devastation comes new purpose, mastery, strategic thinking and another layer added to your "thick skin". You gain the tools to avoid another failure, or at least to face it with the equipment you already have.

What have you learned about yourself in running your business?

When I was five my mother put me into second hand ice-skating boots, put me on the ice and said "Here you go dear, it's your life." Very Russian, isn't it? I made a step and I fell right on my head. I still remember how much it hurt. Shoot, I still have that little bump. I got up, made another step, and fell again. The pain wasn't any easier to bear. I got up again and made another step, but this time I knew how to angle my figure skates. My pride was a bit bruised, but hey, I was standing surely on my two little feet.

I fell many times over, but I learned one thing. If you have to fall, make yourself analyze, calculate and predict where to land. At least bump your butt or your other softer parts, not your head, that damage might be permanent. And always believe that you can pick yourself back up again and get out on the ice to be on the cutting edge of your business.

A lot has been changed since I was five, but I continue constantly learning about myself through the lens of my business and many wonderful people I've been blessed to meet. For example, at the last year Success Summit, national gathering of women entrepreneurs, proved to be the greatest epiphany for many of us, one of the authors and business coaches was standing by the microphone and giving a short introductory speech. Suddenly, she broke into tears. As she was sobbing, she explained that her significant other had been dealing with terminal illness and that experience had been emotionally draining on both of them. I had previously met this gal in person, read her very inspirational book, and at no time did I think she was capable of something like crying, and in public of all places!

Please don't judge me being insensitive at the time. I viewed the ideal businesswoman as an 'iron lady' type of personality. I was also raised in a country where any crying, *especially* in public was perceived as a sign of weakness. Seeing her sob for a moment was a surprise. What was this super achiever and tough cookie doing, crying like a baby in front of other tough cookies?

Later on I couldn't stop thinking about it. It was quietly bugging me for months. I began to question my preconceived notions. After all, I had left my country behind for a reason. I was tired of suppressing my feelings and walking around like a carefully calibrated machine. I finally realized that it's ok to cry and to not be ashamed of your tears. It's ok to be human!

Wow... You can be a business oriented shark and have a softer side below your belt at the same time... what a killer combination. Women entrepreneurs tend to adopt a façade of hardness and steely resolve while we can afford to cry only when nobody looks. While that is certainly impressive, and perhaps perfectly natural, it's equally acceptable to listen to the scared little girl inside of you.

The one is always looking for love, acceptance and sympathy, no matter how old, smart, rich, popular, or successful she is. That's what sets us, women apart as unique type of entrepreneurs; we know that expressing our emotions does not make us less professional, less competent, or less of anything. And of course by telling you this I don't suggest spilling tears to every new client, but I always remind myself not to stop caring for others or yourself just to fit the 'iron lady' mold.

What was your most rewarding experience since starting your own business?

I constantly find myself saying that amazing, intriguing, compelling, rewarding phrase, "Yes, I can!" Those three little words give me so much satisfaction. I can look back proudly at my accomplishments and recognize them as my own backbreaking labor. But I will be perfectly honest with you the money isn't too bad, either.

Your business is like a cow. You raise it right, take care of it you get milk and butter. If not, either you are not fit for the employment of this type or the cow is sick. Evaluate! If the numbers don't work and even if you think that cow has some pretty eyelashes, sell it, get rid of it and buy another cow with less make-up but with more potential and return!.

I've been lucky to raise quite a happy cow thus far and looking around for more.

What 3 things do you now wish you would've known when you started?

1.) First and foremost, no multitasking. We are all mothers, daughters, sisters, wives, partners, you name it. The list of obligations is endless and everybody expects us to serve, provide, comfort, arrange, attend, cater, and do. But at the end of the day, it's about you! You have to serve yourself before you can serve anyone else. Remember when you are on a plane, they instruct you to put that oxygen mask on you first before you can help anybody else around. One thing at a time. Ok, max two...

2.) Reinforce your everyday energy with positive affirmations. That's something I discovered and started to practice just recently. Make yourself wake up on the right foot. So it's **the right one**, not the other one when you start your day. Do NOT put that foot on the floor without you short morning mantra. Something like "it's going to be a great, happy, lucky, prosperous, totally successful day". You can use your own words as long as it gives you energy and radiance to jump out of your bed for this new day to come. Purposely create it! Your sub-conscious will pick up right after.

Developing successful habits is another way to bring positivity into your life, and subsequently your business. Eating healthy, exercising every day, dressing up and wearing high heels might seem exhausting if not ridiculous at times. However, those things are good for you! They are your additional positive affirmations that you're worthy. Taking care of yourself and presenting yourself confidently is that extra boost of "Yes I Can!" thing.

Falling into healthy routines will increase your drive and productivity, not to mention your self-esteem. You also HAVE to spoil yourself a little. Don't be modest here! Get nice clothes and a couple of fancy bags. Throw on some makeup, sneak a peek in a mirror throughout the day reminding yourself how pretty you are. Again, it's not gratification, but a simple affirmation of how good you really are. And you ARE! Have peaceful times for yourself when nobody can get to you (not even your darn-same-song-ringing-his majesty-phone). Quiet your mind. Meditate. Visualize. Breathe... And endlessly LOVE yourself!

3.) However, most importantly, believe. Believe! **Believe in YOU**! You're reading this book so you already do. Don't be afraid of being ambitious and reaching for the top. Your life is a phenomenal and unique luxury car. It has all the bells and whistles that come with a chrome exterior and leather seats, but at its heart is a simple but very powerful GPS. All you really need to do is to program a specific destination and it'll take you there. Clearly see your goal, visualize it every day and stay the path. You don't know what your real top is, so your potential for growth and success is boundless. I've tested it and I know that there're no limits, it's more than you think right now. So believe in a beautiful, healthy, wealthy, and super successful YOU!

What's your biggest business goal over the next 12 months and what will you do to meet it?

The Internet. I really, REALLY want to be friends and partner with this wonderful and cruel thing. When I met that beast for the first time in my life, I honestly wished and prayed it would've died right then and there and left us little people alone! Not happening... Our on-line presence becomes us, as evil as we think it is and this witch isn't going away! So, let's deal with it.

1.) Make sure you have not only have an excellent website but also an excellent website provider. Do a very thorough research of available vendors, make sure they are specializing in your field of business, compare, and ask for outside of your competition references, be extremely selective but don't go cheap. Eventually, it'll hurt you rather than benefit you. Cost does matter here because your return worth it. Been there, done it to save money, failed each time. It's your face so dress it with love, care and class.

2.) Your online visibility. Produce relevant information coming from your heart. They say it's all about "unique content". Of course you can "steal" some of it from other sources, but immediately that damn Google spiders will figure you out and throw you to the tenth page of its searches, area where nobody ever makes it to. Be original, be relevant, be you.

3.) Social media is another Princess we need to wait on hand and foot. As of today, you need to be active on at least five social platforms: Facebook, LinkedIn, Pinterest, Twitter and YouTube depending on your area of marketing. I'm afraid more coming... You probably need between three to four hours a day to maintain and feed Their Majesties, so get separate personnel for it. Outsource. You don't have time for such high-maintenance, so delegate.

4.) Ask for client testimonials. That's apparently our on-line presence future. That's the best way to get your name out, build your reputation and stimulate search engines. Politely ask that your happy clients post something about you and be on review aggregators or their own personal social networks at all times. Monitor your progress and ratings constantly, re-evaluate, adjust, and improve. Try to focus on the creative part of your business rather than competitive.

What advice would you give to a woman entrepreneur who is ready to take her business to the next level?

I remember an old story I heard a long time ago. Once, there was a small village near the woods with hardworking people in it living simple lives. One day a little old lady from that village went to the forest to gather some berries. Suddenly, she stumbled upon a huge hungry wolf with gnashing teeth, ready to attack and eat her up. Imagine the situation!

Huge sharp teeth, no weapon, no physical strength, terrified with fear... just a little old lady and a big, bad wolf. Knowing that she really had nothing to lose, she gathered all her courage. She reached out and grabbed that wolf by the tongue so tight that the poor, shocked thing couldn't even move and grab her anymore. So she dragged that wolf by the tongue all the way to the village where she got help to restrain it only because she knew that it was the end of it if she simply gave up. So COMMITT!

Act like there's no tomorrow and there's no other chance. You've been running on this hamster wheel all your life. You know the rules of engagement by now. But the cool thing is that you can break this cycle and go full speed with a bigger vision of your success. Grab that wild beast by the tongue and don't let go. COMMIT! Yes, you will have nights when you want to curl and cry. You'll have fears, doubts and failures. You will face a number of wolves, some snarling right at you, others waiting in the woods to strike. They'll be younger, smarter, more creative or resourceful, they'll be tall, and they'll be male and not legally blonde… However think about it this way. People who are about to die are often asked what would they do differently with their lives. The answer is always the same: *I wish I hadn't been so afraid or cautious and just gone for it. Why didn't I…* Regret is the great pain that will haunt you like a broken bone that didn't heal quite right. Perhaps you were held back by that old adversary, fear, or you tried something, but did it without commitment. Taking risks is a giant leap of faith, so get prepared, get rid of the regrets and your excess baggage and grab that wolf by the tongue, lady!

Ok, what if you've got to the top and stuck there. You're trying and trying, but something always doesn't let you break that threshold and take your business to another level. How exactly do we deal with that? Or how do you face and resolve crises like with that wolf in the woods? Simple and complicated at the same time.

You have to create effective systems for ongoing development and crisis protection in your business. I'm sure you know and maybe even have seen two super successful shows in Las Vegas. Do Siegfried and Roy and the Blue Man Group ring a bell? Both were great quality productions, both were hugely successful brands with billions of dollars revenue. But there was a crucial difference.

Siegfried and Roy's show was built on a culture of single personality. You came to their show not only for the lions and tigers, but to be charmed by this dynamic duo. That star power kept them on top for decades. Then the unexpected happened, one freaked out or depressed tiger came along and ate Roy, effectively ending their dual reign as the kings of the empire. A multimillion dollar booming profitable structure went down the drain in one minute.

On the other hand, the Blue Man Group gave up individual personalities for a BRAND identity. The members disguise themselves under bald caps and bright blue paint, making one Blue Man pretty damn difficult to distinguish from another not jeopardizing the quality of the product. The unification created a distinct signature, one that is recognizable all over the world. You could easily replace any or all of the members and lose none of the impact. Brutal example, however which system are you using to work your quality product? How will you use your business protection system to avoid or resolve crises?

Any entrepreneur eventually wants one thing – NOT to be your own business' slave. To be able to take vacations, trips, even naps without constantly checking your phone or email, to have quality time with the ones you love, to be free and enjoy your moment and your life at fullest. Just recently I've discovered what a beautiful thing it is, only because I was able to create a team of "blue man" and improve my new business systems. It's been worth every single breath I've taken.

I would like to acknowledge my fabulous, young and talented editor, Anastasia Grinberg. Thank you from the bottom of my heart for taking my rambling and turning it into something understandable! I'm so proud of you.

Continue the Conversation with Larissa Rubijevsky:

It's not about how many homes I've sold or awards I've earned. It's about how many people I've helped to make a difference in their lives.

Larissa
ReMax Estate Properties
Life Achievement and Chairman Club Awards
Platinum Club & Hall of Fame of ReMax International
Top 1% Nationally for Sales, Productivity & Customer Service
Global Marketing Specialist
E-Pro / Quality Service Certified
310 387-1414
www.HomesFromLarissa.com
DRE #1347242

About the Compiler
Kimberly Pitts
Founder of UImpact & Behind Her Brand

Kimberly Pitts is both a Branding & Marketing Strategist and Developer. She is a change agent who is dedicated to helping entrepreneurial women use branding & marketing strategies to position their businesses in the market, attract their target audiences, create influential brands, realize more income, and enjoy freedom in both their businesses and their lives.

She is the proud founder of UImpact, LLC & Behind Her Brand where she helps women entrepreneurs "play big" through her premier training based mastermind program- Thrive Academy, 3D Branding Solutions (Full / Half Day Strategy Sessions), Ignite Your Brand Retreats, and a myriad of ongoing training programs.

Anything but conventional, Kimberly's creative and innovative techniques will challenge you, encourage you, inspire and equip you to get to the place you desire, and deserve to be. Whether you are in the start-up stages of your business or you are ready to grow to the next level of success and expand your reach, Kimberly is here to provide expert coaching and mentoring to better position you and your business for greater influence.

Contact us at:

UImpact, LLC / www.uimpact.net

Behind Her Brand / www.behindherbrand.com

Facebook: www.facebook.com/uimpact

Made in the USA
San Bernardino, CA
28 February 2015